HEILONGJIANG

JILIN

INNER MONGOLIA

LIAONING

JAPAN

Datong

☐ BEIJING

KOREA

HEBEI

SHANXI

SHAANXI

SHANDONG

YELLOW

SEA

Xian

HENAN

JIANGSU

Nanjing

Suzhou

Shanghai

PACIFIC

HUBEI

ANHUI

EAST CHINA

ZHEJIANG

SEA

OCEAN

JIANGXI

HUNAN

FUJIAN

Part I Guangzhou-Beijing

- - - - - - - - - - - -

Part II Beijing-Lhasa

—|—| — |—|—|—|

Part III Lhasa-Kathmandu

——————

JANGXI GUANGDONG

Guangzhou

TAIWAN

Hong Kong

SOUTH CHINA SEA

Haikou

0   100   400

Wanning

miles

anya   HAINAN

100   600   km

Signed by author

Alone through China & Tibet

Helena Drysdale

Alone through China & Tibet

Helena Drysdale
16 October 1986

Constable · London

First published in Great Britain 1986
by Constable and Company Ltd
10 Orange Street London WC2H 7EG
Copyright © by Helena Drysdale
Set in Linotron Ehrhardt 11pt by
Rowland Phototypesetting Ltd
Bury St Edmunds, Suffolk
Printed in Great Britain by
St Edmundsbury Press Ltd
Bury St Edmunds, Suffolk

British Library CIP data
Drysdale, Helena
Alone through China and Tibet
1. China – Description and travel – 1976–
2. Tibet (China) – Description and travel
I. Title
915.1'0458   DS712

ISBN 0 09 467200 8

Contents

Illustrations

between pages 128 and 129

Golmud to Lhasa
The Potala Palace, Lhasa
Prostration before the Jokhang Temple
Prayer wheels in Jokhang's inner courtyard
Old man mumbling prayers
Pilgrims in Drepung
Drepung Gompa
Gyantse Gompa
Pot bellied god, Gyantse

between pages 160 and 161

Typical Tibetan house
Monks restoring Buddha statue, Gyantse
At Gala
Above Gala, looking south
Yaks dressed up for ploughing
Yak dung drying for fuel, Sagya
Tingri East
Thong La

All photographs are by the author, except where otherwise indicated.

Acknowledgements

Special thanks to my mother Merida Drysdale, who has helped me more than she can know, and to Patrick Vandenbruaene.

I am also grateful to the estate of Arthur Waley and Allen and Unwin for permission to quote from *Chinese Poems* translated by Arthur Waley, published in 1948.

Note on transliteration

Throughout this book, Chinese names and terms have been transliterated into the pinyin system, which has been in use in China since 1978, and replaces the older Wade-Giles and Lessing systems. Thus:

Tai Chi	becomes	*Tai qi*
Taoism		*Daoism*
Su Tong-P'o		*Su Dongpo*
Chou En-Lai		*Zhou En Lai*
Canton		*Guangzhou*
Hangchow		*Hangzhou*
Soochow		*Suzhou*
Nanking		*Nanjing*
Peking		*Beijing*
Tatung		*Datong*
Sian		*Xian*
Sinkiang		*Xinjiang*

Pronunciation is basically phonetic, but there are a few idiosyncrasies:

c is pronounced 'ts' as in *its*
q is pronounced 'ch' as in *China*
x is pronounced 'sh' as in *show*
z is pronounced 'ds' as in *bids*
zh is pronounced 'j' as in *jump*
ou is pronounced 'o' as in *woe*

A few familiar names have, however, been retained in their older more familiar forms: Confucius, Sun Yat Sen, and the Yangtze River.

– Part I –

– 1 –
Guangzhou at New Year

I never meant to go to China.

For six months I had been travelling in Asia, and though I was continually aware of the presence of China it was less as a place to visit than as a huge and rather sinister land mass threatening the borders of surrounding countries.

I went to Ladakh to see mountains, temples, Ladakhi people, but found also convoys of khaki army lorries belching black filth into the crisp air, fighter planes, jeeps, and soldiers in the cafés. Though it is over twenty years since the Chinese made their surprise attack over the Himalayas, Ladakh is still a vast Indian military base.

In both Ladakh and Nepal I met Tibetan refugees who in their thousands fled China's so-called 'Liberation' of Tibet in 1959. Many still live in squalid camps, and speak with longing of returning home when their country is free once more. In Burma and Thailand I stayed with the extraordinary Hmong and Karen Hill Tribes who had once lived in China but who have been pushed steadily further and further south by successive repressive regimes.

As I travelled from country to country, skirting round the south of China, so I became more and more intrigued. The Dragon! Dangerous, aggressive, unknown. What was this place that so few people had ventured into, but from which so many have fled? And what was this place that now, after thousands of years, was willingly opening up its doors to the West? Every newspaper I managed to find reported on the latest developments as China heaved itself into the modern world and, as I discovered more, so I felt drawn towards it, and so I realised that this was the perfect moment to go there, when the lives of the people were dramatically changing, but before the immediate past was covered up.

Until then my route had been deliberately unplanned, forged entirely by chance meetings and last-minute decisions. Looking back however, it seems as though my subconscious had been in control and unknowingly I had made plans, and that the purpose of my journey had been, above all, to lead me to China and across the wastelands of the west to Tibet.

However, it did not seem like that at the time, and it was with some surprise, mixed with excitement and trepidation, that I found myself leaving Hong Kong and heading north to Guangzhou (Canton), just in time for the Chinese New Year.

With me were Patrick, a Belgian agronomist I had met in Nepal, and Derek, an enormous black American football player whose formidable bulk was doubled by a large rucksack and half a dozen other bags. We met him at the station; he was going to Beijing to spend a year teaching English. The only 'foreign guests' at the border, we were hustled into a special building to sign forms, change our money into 'Foreign Exchange Certificates', and buy a special (more expensive) foreigners' train ticket: before us was not just another country but an alien world.

With us were hundreds and hundreds of Chinese, squeezing between the crowd barriers to be crushed on to the train; the guard slammed the door shut to hold us in, while others chose the quicker route through the windows. I have never seen a train so full; there were people occupying every available space, on the seats, on each other, on the seat backs, squatting on bags. I blamed the crowds on the celebrations for New Year, but later I discovered that every train on every line at every time of day or night is as packed as this one. At every station in every town there are queues of people waiting for tickets, waiting for trains. One billion people, a third of the world: only after months in China could I begin to comprehend it.

But no one seemed to mind the crowds for this was a festive time, and people smiled at us and offered sweets and were friendly. Most were Hong Kong Chinese returning to their families in south China for the holiday, and their striped nylon bags bulged with presents. Those lucky Chinese with Hong Kong relatives rely on them for supplies of clothing, electrical goods, and other useful things still unavailable in China. They were fascinated by Derek, so huge and so black, (just one of his thighs was the size of a Chinese child's torso) and, to their increasing amazement, able to speak a little Chinese. His every word was imitated, and passed on to family and friends who were too obscured by bodies to see or hear. He began to teach me the Chinese numbers, and soon all around were chanting with us: '*Yi, er, san, si*', and making the appropriate hand gestures and laughing.

No books or photographs could have prepared me for the overwhelming myriad of other impressions as China sprang into being: the roughness of textures, of seat backs and clothes; the gritty floor beneath my feet; the dust along the window sill; the indecipherable mesh of consonants that is Cantonese; and the actual individuals with their multitude of complex reactions to me and mine to them. It is hard to unravel it all now, but what remains above all is an impression of tremendous noise and of being bombarded, swamped. 'I am in China, this is China!' I repeated it to myself in time with the heavy rhythm of the train, trying to believe it.

Through the smeared window I saw the still half-built offices and hotels of Shenzhen, capital of the Shenzhen Special Economic Zone. There are four such zones, designed to attract Western technology and investment. Shenzhen is the very essence of the New China, growing with frightening speed, and said to be their 'silicon valley'. But in just a few minutes we left it behind – the New China had vanished – and found instead blue clothed peasants under wide straw Chinamen's hats, bending to plant rice in the paddy fields between lumpy hills; others balanced on wooden ploughs behind buffaloes; others were on bicycles; and PLA soldiers in baggy green shirts and trousers, red stars gleaming from their caps, hung around at the roadsides. It was all absurdly Chinese.

And on to everything it rained, veils of rain falling interminably from thick, impenetrable skies that gave no hope of ever clearing. At Guangzhou station we surged out into the greyness, grey rain on grey East European buildings, people shrouded in grey plastic raincoats under glistening umbrellas, drops springing from puddled grey tarmac; the only colour was a large hoarding which demonstrated in pinks and greens effective ways of killing rats, and towering above it, the blue and red gleam of neon advertising Sanyo.

I stood there in the rain wondering how my inadequate clothes would keep out pneumonia, and wondering where I should stay, how I should get there, and how I should ask someone these questions. But as the great, wet, crowd surged and buffeted around me, I noticed a small Chinese woman trying to attract my attention.

'Excuse me, are you Australian?'

'No, I'm English.' I was astonished to be addressed in my own language. She had permed hair and seemed anxious.

'Were there any Australians on your train? I'm waiting for two friends, two girls.'

'No, I didn't see any other foreigners. Maybe they'll be on the next train in a few hours.'

She looked around her, then turned back to me and with a hint of conspiracy said, 'If you like, I can take you to the cheapest hotel in Guangzhou – the Government Workers' Hostel, only six yuan a night.'

'But what about your Australian friends?' I asked her.

'Later, later, it doesn't matter,' she replied airily.

I had been joined by Patrick and Derek, and we agreed that her hotel was cheaper than anything else we knew of.

'But what if she's a tout?' I whispered to Derek who had been in China before.

'It's so unlikely,' he said. 'The Chinese just aren't like that, and anyway she is taking us to a government hostel, so she would hardly be touting for that. The last thing they care about is getting business.'

'Anyway,' Patrick added, 'it doesn't matter if she is a tout. What can she do? It's not like Thailand here – I doubt she's going to drug us and steal all our money. Let's just go with her.'

So we sloshed after her across the tarmac to a minibus into which we squeezed ourselves and Derek's luggage.

'My name is Len,' she announced. 'I wish to know you so that I may practise my English. I have been studying for several years at night school.' Her father, she said, was a geography professor and her boyfriend a writer in a government agency.

('That sounds plausible,' Derek whispered. 'You'll find many educated Chinese will go out of their way to help and to practise their English.')

When we reached the hostel Len seemed afraid and refused to come near the entrance, insisting on waiting for us outside in the rain. I felt ashamed of my suspicions.

Despite its uninviting name, the Government Workers' Hostel was quite pleasant, with a dormitory of wide beds covered in mountainous quilts almost too heavy to lift, and on the table several thermoses of boiled water waiting for tea. This, I was to discover, is one of the best things about Chinese hotels: even in the seediest doss house there is always a thermos so no one has to drink impure water. There were also little plastic slippers under the beds for us to paddle about in the watery corridors.

But there was no time to relax: we wanted to see Guangzhou and Len was waiting to show it to us. The hotel itself was on an island – Shamian Island – which, to my surprise, was covered in large European neo-classical buildings faced with yellow and grey stone and surrounding small grassy squares. Appropriately enough, I was staying in what had once been the British and French concession, the only place in Guangzhou where the hated barbarian foreigners were allowed to own land. Here, after defeating the Chinese in the shameful Opium Wars of the mid nineteenth century, the European traders built their headquarters and shipped tea and silk down the Pearl River to Hong Kong and Macau. There was a Catholic church (closed) and small footbridges crossing the canal which divided the island from the mainland: there were no cars and it had a quiet, crumbling charm. But – typical of a developing country – one of the few places tourists might actually want to stay has been dwarfed by the vast slab of the White Swan Hotel, thirty-five storeys high, one of China's newest and most expensive five star hotels with a waterfall in the lobby, a disco, and designer shops.

Downtown, along the riverside in the heart of Guangzhou, the atmosphere could not have been more different. Here the East European blocks were decorated with red and gold New Year greetings, streamers, round red tasselled lanterns. The streets were bustling with walkers, shoppers, fruit sellers, spice stalls, even beggars, all overlooked by the futurist towers of the Renmin (People's) Hotel. Like Christmas in the West, department stores were doing brisk business in clothes*[1], sweets and toys, and couples walking hand in hand paused to look in at the imported cassette players and cameras. Despite the rain it was all much more lively than I had expected, the clothes more colourful and the people more friendly. Restaurants opening off the streets were filled with families, the waiters rushing between round tables bearing aloft plate upon plate of delicious-looking food.

But perhaps most surprising was the black market. All down the street we were pursued by women murmuring 'Change money, change money'. There are two currencies in China, one for foreigners called FEC and one for the people, Renmin

*1. Traditionally at New Year, everyone has a new set of clothes if they can afford it.

bi, (RMB). It is only with FEC that anyone can buy imported Western goods; naturally the Chinese want these goods too, but can only get FEC by changing it for almost twice the amount of RMB on the black market. This means that foreigners (or anyone with FEC) can almost double their money.

'Later, later,' said Len. 'That very dangerous in China,' and she hurried us away with some long and confused tale concerning a policeman disguised as a money changer and a tourist being imprisoned.

I was thankful on my first day in China when everything was so difficult and strange to have someone to show me around and explain these things. She was very kind, and attentive to our every need. On the buses she rushed forward to buy our tickets, and when we handed her the money she waved it away saying 'Later, later, it doesn't matter.' It was the same in the shops: Derek bought some batteries and Len hurried immediately to the cash booth to pay. She, like everyone, was particularly amused by Derek and told us again how happy she was to meet us and to practise her English.

'Tomorrow I want to take you on a proper tour of Guangzhou and then out to the handicraft centre in Foshan. And you, Helena, I am sure you would like to visit the jade factory now and buy some jade?'

'I would like to see some jade, but I don't want to buy anything.'

'What about dinner then? I will take you to a very nice restaurant, very cheap.'

We were not hungry, but were happy to have something small and to buy her dinner. Len seemed thoughtfully aware of our limited budgets as she steered us past all the glittering restaurants on the waterfront to a dank alleyway where we sat on wet plastic chairs cramped on to the pavement under a dripping corrugated plastic roof.

Just behind us dinner was being prepared. A woman picked a live bird out of a box and smashed its head against a stone. Still twitching, it was plucked and gutted. I did not want to offend Len, but I knew I could not stay here long. She however was quite unmoved, and ordered soup, vegetables, fish, crab, meat, rice, noodles. She seemed to be really enjoying herself, tucking into the crab, sucking out the claws, spitting the shell on to the table.

'This very very expensive,' she said cheerfully. 'This the most expensive thing here.'

We three looked at each other and quickly looked away again. We were travellers with empty pockets and Patrick, in particular, had almost nothing; he was beginning to be irritated.

'All I wanted was chicken soup which I ordered ages ago.' So we ordered it again, several times, and eventually it arrived: a deep bowl of grey water with a few lumps of meat suspended in it.

'This tastes strange. Try it.'

I tried it and felt immediate nausea. It was unlike any chicken I had ever tasted, the bones large and round like knuckles not chicken bones. As we left the restaurant we saw what we had really eaten for there in tiny cages beside the cook were hunched two brown owls and several furry racoons.

I walked quickly away down the street, disgusted by what I had seen and eaten, and disgusted by Len for taking us there. All around me food stalls and restaurants took on a new and grotesque aspect and I noticed now what I had blindly walked past before. People were eating kebabs which I now saw were nothing but lumps of animal gut, veins and aortas. Outside a restaurant was a tank in which swam a grey phallus-shaped object like a bottled specimen. On a stall were bowls of wiry black hair. Dangling in the butchers were glistening brown roasted animals about a yard long with muscular legs – they had to be dogs. I was to see worse in the notorious Qingping market: pangolins, monkeys, snakes, long black rubbery cow's stomach, pig's feet. Chinese food is famine food, and after years of starvation nothing is wasted and every part of every animal is eaten.

'We had better sort out the bill for that dinner.' The others had joined me. Once again, Len had rushed forward to pay, but it was only now when we saw to our dismay how much, that we realised at last what she had been doing. She did not want to practise her English or to give us a taste of Cantonese cuisine, but to change money herself on the black market in a more clever way than the women on the street. She had been getting FEC from us on a one-to-one basis by urging us to spend money, paying for things herself in people's money and then getting us to give her the same amount in FEC. We felt absurd and foolish and cheated, picked up directly from the station before we had had a chance to discover anything. Presumably Len waited there every day for innocents like us. Odd remarks came back to me: she had mentioned wanting to buy an English typewriter, and of course there was the long story about the policeman. Now she had given us a bill which was more than twice what it should have been. We were staggered; Len, we decided, would have to pay some of it herself. Now she, too, was upset. Suddenly she was no longer interested in our tour of Guangzhou, or in taking us out to Foshan. No, she had suddenly quite lost interest in us, and could not wait to leave us. The whole affair was embarrassing and pitiful. We walked back to the street women and changed our money at the best rate we could get.

Compared with the West there is little other crime in China and that same evening I saw why. Outside a 'cultural park' (a fairground) people were gazing at some noticeboards; I peered over their shoulders to see a number of photographs, black and white mugshots of men and women with cropped hair and frightened faces. Without being able to read the captions I knew immediately what these were. Another photograph showed a football stadium in which stood a row of people with their hands tied behind their backs and heads bowed. Behind them stood a row of policemen and beside, a pile of bicycles, TV sets and cassette recorders. Beneath this another mugshot of a man was crossed by a red line. Since 1983 thousands of petty criminals from all over China have been given mass trials in stadiums and then have been executed.

It was not gunfire, however, that ricocheted off the walls with deafening violence that first night and for the next two weeks, but firecrackers. Though it was still several days before New Year, the excitement was building up and firecrackers exploded and spluttered all day and late into the night, frightening off evil spirits and shedding red confetti on to the pavements. But the brutality and superstition that still lie at the heart of Chinese society are fused with a great delicacy, and at every corner were flower sellers with branches of blossoming peach trees[*1], bunches of chrysanthemums and stalls selling mounds of kumquats, golden symbols of wealth.[*2]

Over those next few days Patrick and I visited museums, temples, parks, exhibitions, walked miles down pretty tree-lined back streets of red brick houses, and squeezed into double jointed buses. Many things were closed for repairs or simply closed, and always the rain fell, cascading off tin roofs, curling round bicycle tyres. It was bitterly cold and we argued outside the Sun Yat Sen Memorial Hall, made up at the Five Storey Pagoda, fought again at the hideous Sculpture of the Five Rams. Our clothes were never dry, and there was nowhere to get warm; we did not want to waste the day in our dormitory, but restaurants were not much of a refuge, mostly big and open-fronted, with rain splashing on to the oilcloths and the floor. Once or twice we retreated to the draughty corridors of the huge and once grand Dongfeng Hotel to let rain stream off us in 'Food Street' and 'Gourmet Gallery' as we drank cup after cup of hot jasmine tea.

But my spirits were never dampened for long; the closures and the rain and the arguments really did not matter for they were a part of China and in those early days everything – Len, the hotel, the firecrackers, the flowerstalls, everything –

[*1]. Peach wood is used to keep away evil spirits.
[*2]. In Cantonese, kumquat puns with the word for gold.

seemed fantastical and bizarre and fascinating. I was in a dream in which most things were recognisable – houses, restaurants, shops – yet in some way distorted. Or it was like looking at life through cross eyes, or from upside down, standing on my head, everything slightly askew. For a few minutes I would forget where I was and begin to accept things as normal, but then I would remember, 'I am in China!' and it all became fantastical again.

But I was desperately frustrated by my inability to speak the language and discover how the ordinary Cantonese people viewed their changing world. Until we met Mr Xie, that is. Patrick and I hired bicycles from an enterprising old man who had set himself up in a private rental business opposite the hostel and we cycled off to visit the Hinhua temple. We lost our way several times, and finally stopped at the roadside to study the map again.

'May I help you?' A middle-aged man looked earnestly at us through thick round glasses. We explained.

'Oh, I know the temple well, though it must be over ten years since I visited it. Follow me, I'll take you there.'

He led us through a maze of tiny streets which opened out into a small peaceful courtyard where crumbling grand houses tried to maintain their dignity behind the underwear that dangled from every balcony. In one corner was the temple, recognisable from afar by its curving tiled pagoda roof. But as we came closer we saw that apart from the roof there was nothing of this temple left. It had become a print factory.

'I am so sorry,' our new friend apologised. He was deeply ashamed, but hastened to reassure us. 'During the Cultural Revolution so many things disappeared, but now, since the Gang of Four were smashed life is improving again, and the ancient temples and monuments are being restored.'

'Since the Gang of Four were smashed': how many times I was to hear that phrase. The Gang of Four are the scapegoats, this is the official line. Now that the Gang of Four have gone, everything will be all right.

We strolled back through the streets together and Mr Xie ('Mr Thankyou in your language') continued, 'A madness gripped the people, including myself, during the Cultural Revolution, but it was all a mistake. When the Cultural Revolution erupted, I left school and instead of going on to further studies I became a worker in a factory.'

'What happened afterwards?'

'I stayed there for eight years until after the madness was over, and then I went as an older student to Canton University. Now I am an English teacher.'

The full range of horrors perpetrated by the Red Guards and Cultural Revolutionaries is still being assessed. I was reading volumes of Chinese short stories, the first published in 1978 as part of a genre known as 'Scar Literature' which derives from a story called 'The Scar', about the wounds inflicted by the Gang of Four. Seven years later, these wounds had still not healed and were the source for most of the recent stories.

These stories were published by the government as part of their anti-Gang-of-Four propaganda, but there is no denying the reality of the pain expressed, and I was surprised by Mr Xie's frankness in admitting his own involvement in inflicting that pain. Though I longed to know more, I did not want to press him, and he was not forthcoming. Nevertheless, when we arrived back at our bicycles he seemed keen to continue our conversation and invited us home to see his baby. Whether through fear of being watched by his street committee or through genuine modesty about his house, I do not know; in any case, he did not at first invite us inside.

'Wait here,' he said when we reached the small yard where he lived, and he disappeared into a dilapidated building to return proudly with his wife carrying their smiling round ball of a little girl. In her flowery red and yellow trousers she seemed to have drained all the colour and beauty from her parents, leaving them grey and drab.

As we admired her the rain began again and Mr Xie came visibly to a decision.

'Perhaps you would like to come in for a while? But please forgive me,' he apologised several times, 'our home is so small and untidy.'

It was in a large old brick town house, barred at the entrance by a sort of horizontal portcullis and now divided into narrow high-ceilinged flats. We were led up chilling stone steps into what did indeed seem a tiny, cramped and icy cold room with dark-grey painted walls and a bare stone floor. There were a few other rooms opening off it so perhaps by Chinese standards it was considered spacious, but to me it was a house in which some pathetic Dickensian weaver might have lived.

However, the welcome was warm from Mr Xie's old mother who seemed not in the least surprised to see us, and immediately produced tea, oranges, pumpkin seeds, fried prawn crackers and a flat tin of strange grey jelly. Neither Patrick nor I could manoeuvre this jelly on to our chopsticks so, specially for the foreign guests, a plastic fork was produced. Patrick tried once again with the jelly and promptly snapped the fork in half. He blushed. 'I am terribly sorry.'

'It doesn't matter, it doesn't matter,' cried Mr Xie, and when his wife left for work as a shop assistant, he begged us to stay longer.

The little girl was put in a play-pen beside us, and old Mrs Xie showed us photo albums filled with colour pictures of the beloved grandchild with her parents, her every gesture and expression captured and doted over. Under the one-child family system, this is the only child they will have. Since the late 1970s the government has been trying to reduce the population by promoting its one-child campaign with posters in every town, with late marriages, easily available contraception, sterilisation, late abortions. If a couple sign a contract agreeing to have only one child they are given money, better housing, promotion at work and other benefits. If they break the contract they lose the privileges and are heavily penalised. It was rumoured that a no-child campaign was about to start.

For centuries before 'Liberation', to give birth to a girl was considered a misfortune. A boy was a gift from heaven, someone to help in the fields or to be educated into the civil service; a girl was nothing but a financial drain, useless with her little bound feet, and someone to be married off as soon as possible. Unless she had bound feet, no husband would look at her. 'How sad it is to be framed in woman's form', wrote Fu Hsuan in the third century. 'Nothing on earth is held so cheap. A boy that comes to a home drops to earth like a god that chooses to be born. His bold heart braves the Four Oceans, the wind and dust of a thousand miles. No one is glad when a girl is born; by *her* the family set no store.' There was little change for 1,500 years. In poor peasant households mothers were often forced to part with this extra mouth, and girls were given away as servants or sold, some joined opera troupes, others were sent away as concubines. I read in the *China Daily*, the English language newspaper, sad advertisements by women seeking to be reunited with their families who were probably separated in this way.

'I am seeking my mother Ms Kuang Meiqin, sixty, and I'm looking for my sister Ms Ye Li'e, forty . . .'.

But even now, so many years after the 1950 New Marriage Law that gave equal rights to men and women, most couples want their only child to be a boy, and female infanticide in some remote rural areas is a recognised problem. So the campaign posters always show a smiling happy couple with their rosy-cheeked daughter.

But girl or boy, the only child is the most treasured member of society, encased in a special baby side-car beside its parent's bicycle, or wheeled along in a little go-cart to nursery school, the bigger ones waddling behind clinging to a rope. Many are dressed in miniature army uniforms with soldiers' Mao caps on their heads, but lower down their fat bare bottoms poke out through the split in their trousers. Some are so well-padded against the cold behind gloves and scarves and woolly hats that their black eyes and pink bottoms are the only bits to be seen. Maybe it is because babies wear split trousers and no nappies that they never cry. Not once in China did I hear a baby cry.

For several hours we sat in that dark cold room. We talked about painting and Mr Xie said his favourite Western art was Impressionism. 'Nevertheless,' he added, 'painting should reflect the society from which it comes, so landscape painting is better when there are figures in it.' I thought of the Yuan, Jaio and Fen notes, FEC and RMB, the latter showing landscapes filled with sturdy workers with uplifted rejoicing faces, sitting on tractors or striding into the fields, while the tourist money, pandering to decadent Western tastes, shows beautiful classical Chinese landscapes entirely free of figures.

This led me to another thought. There is no question of what art ought to reflect: there is no morality in art. But perhaps all art does, despite itself, in some way reflect the society from which it comes. I had seen an exhibition of new sculpture by young Chinese artists, all of it figurative and displaying the most trite forms of Western art: serpentine ladies, moon-eyed girls, fluorescent autumnal landscape. I wondered if this reflected the society from which it came, a society racing towards the most easily accessible products of the West – fast food, television with its consumer-orientated American-style game shows, and Western music. I asked Mr Xie if he thought China could cope with all this. 'Why not?' he cried. 'We can take the good things from the West and leave the bad like pornography. In any case, things always work out for the best. Man always finds the best for himself.'

I looked around his gloomy house and thought of the upheavals in his life, and admired his optimism (optimism being the mark of a good communist). He continued, 'The West seems to worry that the reforms in China will not last after the death of Deng Xiaoping, but they will last because the wish for reform comes from the people. The government is simply the mouthpiece of the people. Things are moving slowly, and though there is better housing, there is still unemployment. But why not? At least now, since the Gang of Four were smashed, the state automatically employs university graduates. We call that the "iron rice bowl" – unbreakable. Your system of unemployment benefit is another kind of iron rice bowl. These young university graduates are now replacing the old guard of uneducated peasants and also, in some industries, anyone over the age of fifty. My uncle, for example, is over fifty and does not have a degree so he must leave his position as the head of an engineering project even though this project has improved under his leadership.'

'Isn't that a bit hard for him?'

'Yes it is, I must admit, but you can't make exceptions, and he will continue to receive the same wages.'

We talked until we were stiff with cold about the relationship between China and Europe, about Western religions and Taijiqian, and about the lack of world news and English language publications in China. He subtly criticised the simplistic propaganda of the *China Daily*. Mr Xie did have an English magazine called the *Picture Scientist* which the grandmother handed to the little girl. The grandmother went away and I, sitting nearest the play pen, did not notice that the child was ripping up the pages.

'Oh it doesn't matter, it doesn't matter,' cried Mr Xie again, endlessly courteous. But despite his offer of a 'simple lunch of noodles' we decided it was time to leave. He brought the child out to see us off, and waving goodbye and promising to write, we rode away.

That evening, down in the shadowy places along the embankment where black humps on the benches were couples kissing, Patrick told me that he wanted to stay in China only for about ten days.

'But why? We've only just arrived.'

'You know why.'

We were sitting on a step in the dark; time was punctuated by a stream of silhouetted figures that poured over a bridge at regular intervals.

'Yes, I know why.'

'I have to go back and see her again so as to be sure. I can't bear to write, and I can't leave her waiting for me any longer.'

'So what will you do?'

'I'll stay in the south for a while and then head north to take the trans-Siberian from Beijing back to Belgium ... What about you?'

I had known these words would be said ever since we first met. That we knew it was going to end like this had originally been at the heart of our glorious freedom together. But things had changed and I had come to dread this moment. What would I do? Suddenly the future loomed up against me like a blank wall that I strained to see over but could not. What will I do? Go back to Hong Kong too, and look for a job there? But I hated the pushy glamour of Hong Kong and knew I could not stay there. Go with him on the trans-Siberian? That would hardly be tactful, and anyway I had no desire to return to Europe yet. Stay on, alone, in China? Alone, in this vast alien place: I felt dwarfed by the prospect and frightened. But I had only just arrived and there was so much I wanted to see; and I despised myself for being afraid. I looked at him.

'I'm going to stay on in China.'

I could always change my mind.

It was New Year's Eve, and the corner stalls with their striped awnings had swallowed up whole streets to sell flowers, oranges, miniature kumquat trees and other golden good luck symbols – goldfish. Bicycles wobbled away under pear tree branches crammed into their back baskets, and steadily more and more people arrived, buying, selling, shouting, singing; bands were playing, marching tunes strode forth out of loud-speakers and firecrackers crackled. Even the deluge of freezing rain could not drown the excitement, and at two a.m. the following morning the market would still be open.

But it was at midnight, when at last our hotel was quiet and everyone in the dormitory asleep, that there came the real burst of enthusiasm. Suddenly the whole city exploded into one giant firecracker, erupting from every window, clattering down walls and along passageways, the air thick with acrid smoke. It was like being under fire, and we all ran to the windows, hopping about in our strange assortment of long johns and vests that served as pyjamas. A Spaniard, Salvatore, filled tea cups with brandy, and Derek broke up a few red-bean buns, and shouting above the noise we toasted in the Year of the Ox.

The firecrackers started again before dawn but on New Year's Day the centres of activity were the temples. New Year is their busiest time when the gods must be propitiated in the hope they will reward the faithful with a year of prosperity. At the Buddhist Temple of the Six Banyan Trees with its seventeen storey pagoda people were lighting joss sticks (*joss* meaning luck in Chinese) and sticking them into a sand-filled incense burner. The air was filled with their sweetish scent. In a small temple behind the pagoda the faithful jostled to bow down on their knees to the Buddha and the fat golden Maitreya or future Buddha who looks so happy about his prospects. A grey coated monk, with a shaven head and grey breeches over grey knee-length boots, was sitting beside a lacquered red pillar inscribing prayers in exchange for a little money.

This temple is the centre of Buddhism in Guangzhou, particularly venerated since Bodhidharma, the founder of Chan (Zen) Buddhism, is said to have spent a night here. Indian monks such as Bodhidharma, some accompanying Indian merchants, are supposed to have been the channel along which Buddhism spread to China from the third century BC onwards.

Instead of ousting the already established Confucianism and Daoism, Buddhism intermingled with them to 'flow into one' and to give the practical Chinese the benefit of more gods and spirits, and also safeguards for the hereafter. The apparent contradictions between these philosophies were dismissed, and temples are shared. Su Dongpo, the Song dynasty scholar-official, painter and poet visited the temple in the eleventh or twelfth century and was so enchanted that he gave it this name, but the banyan trees have long since gone.

Near the temple a group of children held up whirring plastic windmills. We followed them into a courtyard which turned out to be another much older temple, built like a traditional Chinese house with courtyards enclosed by long low buildings, each courtyard opening into the next. I discovered later that it had indeed been a Chinese house, in the second century BC, built to accommodate all the members of the family as it grew – husbands, wives, concubines, children, grandchildren. Families lived together in this way for several thousand years.

Here joss sticks were lit in bundles, rolls of paper flamed and smoked in a carved bronze urn, and incense billowed from openings in a lidded pot. Through the haze a column of people swarmed up some steps towards a lantern-hung temple, across the façade and down again, their beetling flow accompanied by the low droning of their prayers. It was a fabulous choreographed dance, an operatic chorus, and I half expected a great bass voice to thunder forth.

We too were swept up into the temple, face to face with two tall golden gods with long black beards: Confucius. For this was the Bright Filial Piety Temple, filial piety being one of the fundamental Confucian laws governing human relationships, the respect of son for father, of younger brother for elder brother, of wife for husband, of younger for elder, and of subject for ruler. This is the concept of *Li* meaning propriety and ritual on which life – if there is to be well-being – should be based. Propriety, ritual, human dignity in daily life, in a ruler, in a government, in civilisation: these are the Confucian ingredients of a well-balanced life. Though his teachings are so deeply rooted in man and his relationships, Confucianism was made a state religion during the Han dynasty (206 BC–220 AD), and Confucius himself is worshipped.

The incense stung our eyes and we moved on to a darker temple where an altar before another array of deities was laden with offerings of oranges, nuts, cakes and sweets. This was the

Hall of the Sleeping Buddha who, it is thought, if sufficiently bribed can cure infertility. I had never expected to see the temples so active. Under the new more liberal regime a certain amount of religious freedom is allowed, though this is largely for the benefit of tourism. I watched a man wearing a red armband – a Party representative – walk casually up to the offerings, rummage through to find a sweet he liked, unwrap it and eat it.

– 2 –

To Hainan Island

We could bear Guangzhou's cold and ceaseless rain no longer and decided to leave for the sun. Hainan Island off the south-west coast was the furthest south we could go, on the same latitude as northern Thailand and central Burma: surely we should find warmth there. Officially only the capital city of Haikou was open to foreigners, perhaps because the island is a military base close to Vietnam, but China was opening up so fast and rules were changing so often, that we decided to risk the two-day bus journey. The draw not only of sun and sea but also of the chance to explore the Chinese countryside was stronger than any doubts.

So at 4.30 in the morning we chalked up a farewell message to Derek on the hotel blackboard and crept outside. With plastic raincoats over ourselves and our packs we looked like two enormous hunchbacks looming through the still dark streets. Even at that hour we were not alone: shifts were changing and people going to and from work were standing silently at the dark bus stops. In the bus station families rolled up in blankets amongst their baggage and the puddles, and people sitting dully on long wooden benches waited for their buses home after the family reunions. Sometimes husbands and wives are sent to work at opposite sides of the country, and this is one of the few times they can meet.

Our bus was of course packed with people and bags, three passengers on one side and two on the other on tiny cramped seats with no leg room. But at least this way we all stayed warm and the compression of bodies kept us on the seats as we crashed over pot-holes. Beside us was a young man also going to Hainan who throughout the day pressed on us handfuls of melon seeds, tangerines, bunches of finger-long bananas, and refused anything in return. Time and again I met such simple, open friendliness as this.

After several hours we drew up in a muddy yard and everyone rushed off the bus. Unsure of what was happening, we followed them to find a draughty barn in which they were crowding round a canteen fighting for bowls of rice and meat. We were not hungry but everyone gestured us over, concerned that we should eat.

All day long we prayed the clouds would lift as we progressed slowly south-west. Mountain ridges, we hoped, would catch the clouds and free the sun but no, we remained shrouded in a murky blur as dark as at dawn. We did pass some fascinating villages however, dominated by mansions like Italian villas with Chinese roofs but all now empty and ruined. Some were towers, often three or four in each village, doubtless competing for height as in a Chinese San Giminiano. I was surprised that after forty years these visible reminders of the old feudal landlords and rich peasants were still left standing. Perhaps they had been the country retreats of wealthy Cantonese merchants who wore embroidered silks and grew their finger-nails into talons protected behind silver shields, and did business with the British while plotting their downfall.

Around the towers clustered the meagre brick dwellings which had been the homes of serfs who, if they could not pay their rents and feudal dues were forced to borrow money at such extortionate interest rates – usually from those same landlords – that they were enslaved for ever. The other crippling expenses were a daughter's wedding, and a funeral. I looked around at the people on the bus and thought that for all their poverty, for all their servitude to the state, and for all the succession of disastrous economic policies, their lives must have improved.

Several times we broke down, and once stopped for two hours in a freezing bus station. While the engine was repaired we all crouched together in a disused bus, trying to keep warm in a fug of cigarette smoke. Eventually at midnight we reached Zhanjiang near the south coast, and here we stopped for the night. Someone pointed us in the direction of the hotel, and we found a grey concrete block built like most modern Chinese architecture either by Soviet architects in the 1950s or according to Soviet designs. Wind pushed through swing doors and along cavernous echoing corridors. After much persuasion we were given a room: two lumpy beds, dust-covered curtains tied in knots, and on the floor a half-filled chamber pot. People shouted and banged doors and let off firecrackers as we sat there cold and tired and damp: melancholy descended on us. Out in the hallway we followed some hissing pipes to a flooded steamy bathroom, and filled a bowl with boiling water in which to warm our feet.

For a long time I lay awake and wondered how it would be when I was alone. Days of travelling, nights in empty forgotten towns – they would be hard to bear. On and off, it was four months that Patrick and I had been travelling together, ever since he came to my rescue in Nepal. I had collapsed with dysentery and ended up on an intravenous drip in the Government hospital, a terrible place: breeze block bunkers under corrugated iron roofs standing in a field. There were no nurses, no drugs, no sheets to cover the black plastic mattresses, just a solitary Korean missionary doctor whom Patrick helped to unearth. A neon light cast its greenish glow on the draped cobwebs and on the coughing twig-thin Nepalese encamped on and around the other beds. Though we had met only a few days earlier, Patrick then went back and forth to the market to buy the prescribed drugs (waiting while the chemist finished his card game) and fetched me his sleeping sheet to separate my fevered body from the clammy plastic. When I despaired and decided to leave Asia and return home, Patrick encouraged me to stay on.

So I did, and recovered enough to spend one month trekking with him in the Himalayas following trails made by Nepalese porters through a part of the world where there are no roads. At night we lodged with the villagers, sleeping on wooden boards in barns (mice scuttling along the rafters) or simply on the floor around their fire. Patrick and I shared so much – the beauty of the stepped paddy fields and the black and orange sunrise on Macchepuchare, the agony of climbing the Thorong Pass before descending into the deepest valley in the world – that inevitably we grew closer. Yet he would return to his world and I to mine, he would return to his girl friend and I would continue on around the world alone and unhindered. Because there was no future for us there was no need to criticise or to judge; we could just be ourselves, together but free. That at least was the theory.

But as I lay on that damp and lumpy bed in Zhanjiang and a firecracker sporadically clattered and drilled, I knew we were not just happy-go-lucky travellers keeping each other company before going our separate ways. This was what we had hoped to be, but it was not the case. We dreaded parting. Though I longed to travel alone again, to be self-sufficient and to take risks for myself and be challenged by loneliness, I could not bring myself to leave. I think it was the same for him. We despised ourselves for not breaking away, but what could we do? We were in love.

> Out in the bushlands a creeper grows,
> The falling dew lies thick upon it.
> There was a man so lovely,
> Clear brow well-rounded.
> By chance I came across him,
> And he let me have my will.
>
> Out in the bushlands a creeper grows,
> The falling dew lies heavy on it.
> There was a man so lovely,

Well-rounded his clear brow.
By chance I came across him:
'Oh, Sir, to be with you is good.'

[Seventh century BC]

The continuing drizzle and cold, and what little we had
already seen of the city did not entice us out of bed in the
morning; in fact we did not emerge until about 2.30 in the
afternoon. We heard the beating of a drum and ran outside in
the hope that it was the Chinese dragon we had failed to see in
Guangzhou but it was only a sad collection of men swaying
along under a cloth lion topped by a piece of tinsel, and some
children unenthusiastically waving red flags, a dreary sight in
these wide grey deserted boulevards. Patrick tried to feel
excited and took a photograph while I turned away to find
myself being stared at by an old man whose expression was the
essence of amazement and horror: mouth hanging open, eyes
wide. I stared back, but realised that I must be the more curious
sight. Pulled down over my ears like a helmet was a grey
woollen Chinese hat; on my hands serving as gloves, a pair of
socks, and around my neck bulging under the plastic mac like a
goitre, a pair of tracksuit bottoms.

The procession trailed off and the street subsided into grey
boredom once more. Zhanjiang was supposedly a major naval
base and port, under French control until 1939 and now the
centre of the foreign-backed oil drilling industry, but this was
all on the other side of town across several miles of wasteland.

But, typical of many Chinese towns, in behind the blocks
and the boulevards was a lively old quarter, its warren of
narrow cobbled streets lined with twisted tree trunks like the
back streets of a southern European town.

The houses were mostly two storeys high and whitewashed,
but desperately cramped, just one room partitioned by a thin
board. Walls and floors were bare with nothing to provide
comfort or warmth, though some had radios and black and

white televisions and two houses had been decorated from floor to ceiling with postcards and of course the red and gold New Year characters. But it was dark, and despite the poverty these little streets and candle-lit houses took on a magical charm as the dragon's drum passed by and fireworks sputtered. A tiny open-fronted shop sold cigarettes and jars of sweets, and we were surrounded by the smiling family who called to the others at the back of the shop to come out and see us. We bought a few things but they gave us more, and they were greatly amused by our faltering Chinese.

The wider streets were full of people and brightly-lit shops selling mounds of spices and ginseng and other roots. Inevitably we lost our way; we had no idea where our hotel was or even what it was called. If we could get to the Northern bus station we could find our way back from there, so a woman kindly left her shop and led us back through the streets, only to find it was the wrong bus station. After more enquiries, and more helpful and curious people gathering round, we were led back the opposite way, but it was no good, none of us seemed to have any sense of direction. Finally, growing desperate, we asked a soldier who was buying cigarettes. Yes, he knew the hotel, and would give us a lift there. He waved towards the road and there, purring in wait, was his large black car, the only car I had seen in Zhanjiang and minutes later we were back at the hotel.

– 3 –

Haikou: the capital

We were brutally woken at 5 a.m. by a banging on the door and switching on of the light: it was time for our onward bus to Hainan. After several hours we offloaded on to a wide dock to join hundreds of Chinese queuing for boats across the Qiong-zhou Strait. Beside us were two primitive-looking men smoking *bongs*, bamboo pipes over two feet long, their possessions in two baskets which hung from poles across their shoulders. I guessed they were not Han Chinese but Hmong (Miao) people, so similar were they to the refugees in the Banvinai Hmong refugee camp where I had stayed in Thailand. Those people had originally come from China but had been pushed south to Laos where they now face reprisals for working for the CIA during the Vietnam war, and so have been forced to flee south again. They are animist and outside their villages in Thailand set up elaborate and delicate bamboo constructions to trap the good spirits and keep out the bad ones. They are also polygamists and opium growers; they are smaller than the Hans and the men in particular have slightly half-witted in-bred looks.

Those that remained in China form one of about fifty-five 'minority groups', which include Tibetans and Mongolians, altogether less than 7 per cent of the population but spread over 50 per cent of the country. Each group have their own traditional beliefs, customs, and dress (though these two men wore utilitarian Chinese clothing) but share their traditional oppression by the Han majority. Until the revolution the characters for 'minority' included the sign for 'dog': only afterwards was it changed to 'man'. It is the Hong and Li minorities who inhabit central Hainan, and for this reason Hainan is an Autonomous Region, aministered at a slight distance from central government. It is not known exactly why they have been given this privilege – perhaps to appease them for earlier Han wrongdoings, or else to reward them for helping the Communists during the Civil War.

The boat crossing was a short one, only two hours, but it was a journey I shall never forget. Almost before we had left the harbour, people were leaning over the railings and vomiting into the sea. As we got going the railings and the sea were ignored, and people stayed in their seats and leant forward to vomit on whatever was in the way. A man sitting opposite me passed most of the journey with his finger up his nose, others spat, others dribbled, until the floor was awash. We began to get hysterical as Patrick pointed out one horror after another and all the time, throughout the two hours, a young man jigged from foot to foot, on and on without ceasing until we reached Haikou.

Haikou harbour was scruffy, but sailing shakily past a dockyard lined with new cars and a factory pumping out smoke, was a junk in full sail, the first I had ever seen, as unwieldy as an old tattered bird. It was a strange juxtaposition of new and old, and one which became for me a symbol of the island for, having expected a forgotten, backward, minorities' place, I discovered that Hainan had now been declared a Special Economic Zone, like Shenzhen, with tax concessions, special import-export licences, and plans for large scale development in tourism.

So as the minority people shouldered their baskets and half-walked, half-jogged under them into the town, roaring past them came the latest Mitsubishi vans. We reached the hotel to find not a decrepit lodge but a glittering palace, still half-built, with chandeliers, uniformed receptionists, carpets, two restaurants, and a huge Friendship store selling Hong

Kong imports. There were also gangs of Hong Kong Chinese in their colourful padded sportswear, for this is to be the new Hong Kong holiday resort. Along the street were more Friendship stores selling Japanese TVs, music centres, Honda motor bikes, and cosmetics, and more shops were in the process of being built. Outside the hotel, boys clustered like insects around Space Invader machines. Safely offshore, the island is an *in vitro* experiment in capitalism.

Only a few hundred yards away was the old town, the contrast between the two even more extreme than in Zhanjiang. The new town, though bursting with the latest products, was architecturally drear and inhuman while the old city, once quite elegant but now decaying, was full of life in the teahouses and filthy restaurants.

Several streets were taken over by the market in which stalls sold every sort of dried fish, squid, sharks' fins, nuts, noodles, roots, dried fruits, cheap clothes, pearls, baskets. There were barely-live turtles in red plastic buckets, and pigs squeezed into long wicker tubes through which poked their trotters and their snouts. They were heaved off the backs of bicycles on to a pile of other pigs, to be unceremoniously hauled up on hooks, weighed, prodded, and then dumped down again. The pigs were squealing in terror, the whites of their eyes glinting, and not surprisingly for just behind was the abattoir from which their friends' blood flowed. Ranged along a stall were the parts of the carcass, and every part is sold. Two men grasped a pig's head to scrape off the skin, and later I saw that same head sticking out of a shopping bag.

Next came the chickens: a woman briskly wiped her knife on the feathers and then sliced off their heads, holding them upside down over soup bowls to catch the blood. This too is sold. Some kittens were in a cage, and on inquiring if they were for eating, I was answered with a curt nod. Of course they were for eating. In the West we are shielded from the more repulsive aspects of killing and eating; in China it is so much a part of everyday life that the squeamishness of shoppers or any sentimentality over the welfare of animals simply do not exist. Animals are nothing more than matter, to be used, and I tried to accept this. But much later I was to see the Pandas in Beijing zoo – animals being used in another way, to make money. Outside the Panda house were stalls and stalls selling Panda toys, Panda T-shirts, Panda books, every sort of Panda memorabilia; inside were pathetic moth-eaten creatures crouching beside a radiator in a room the size of a prison cell. No attempt had been made to re-create their natural environment. At that moment in Beijing zoo I hated the Chinese.

Close to the market were the now familiar photographs of mass trials, but there were also horrific photos of traffic accidents that serve as warnings to cyclists and drivers. Nothing had been left to the imagination.

Another street, and there was the medicine man who sat beneath a sheet which, spread out across a wall, depicted every kind of hideous internal organ afflicted with a variety of diseases, and ranged over the grass in front of him was every possible cure: snake skins, tortoise shells, roots and mounds of earthy powders and brown potions, one of which he recommended for the cold I was getting.

Side by side, this world and the new packaged world of the Friendship stores must coexist, and I wondered how these people – the medicine man, the woman beheading chickens – could suddenly assimilate cosmetics and motor bikes and modern Western values. I feared for China, and particularly for Hainan. Yet assimilation does take place, and here already a sort of hybrid mix of old and new, of Chinese and Western, was growing up. At the hotel there was a disco, and at the disco all the latest Western hits were played, yet the Chinese were dancing the two-step, and the men were dancing with the men and the women with the women – a hangover of prudery from the Cultural Revolution. In the smart hotel dining-room the floor was carpeted, but this did not deter the Chinese from spitting on it, as normal; up on the roof in the glamorous penthouse bar, looking over the city lights and the harbour, there wafted up the familiar smell of drains: it was all quite reassuring.

From time to time the authorities clamp down when the speed of change has outrun the people themselves, and from the moment we arrived in Haikou we knew there must be a scandal. The black market was rife, the money changers in a token disguise as cigarette sellers. A Hong Kong business man told us he had telephoned the mayor to find out the latest dollar exchange rate, and the mayor had replied 'it depends on which exchange rate you mean'. Then there were the mysterious car parks, lined with imported Japanese cars, Mitsubishi, Toyota, all new but disguised under layers of dust. We had seen these same dust-covered cars hidden in the hotel courtyard in Zhanjiang, and now here they were behind the bus station, along the docks, behind building sites – everywhere. It was obvious then that some sort of illegal business was going on, and only a few months after I left China a massive corruption racket was exposed. These cars were being sold to the mainland at a huge profit for the cadres (as the bureaucrats are known). Several of them were subsequently removed and, it is rumoured, executed.

Day by day the weather deteriorated further: it was still raining and colder than ever. We were unable to force ourselves outside, and as far as we knew we had seen all there was to see. So we sat alone in the gloomy dining-room while waitresses prepared tables for the next meal, and felt our spirits sink with the temperature. We were not hopeful about getting to the south of the island where we might find the sun as the guide book had this to say:*The long distance bus station will* not *sell you tickets to travel outside Haikou unless you have a permit from Public Security, and of course Public Security will not give you a permit.* Moreover, the continuous fighting between China and Vietnam had recently escalated, and it was along the coast of the island that many of the Chinese naval bases lay. Perhaps our journey here would, after all, prove futile.

But eventually we hauled ourselves out of our lassitude and

tried to leave the town. We asked the hotel receptionists but they had no idea what we were trying to say.

'Excuse me, may I help you?' A young Chinese man smiled politely. He was wearing a smart green raincoat and full length green rubber boots, and he had his hair swept forward from the back of his head in a way peculiar to many Chinese men.

'Oh! You speak English?' I was surprised because he looked so young and, judging from his appearance, was not from Hong Kong.

'Yes,' he explained, 'I am a student preparing for entrance examinations to Beijing Foreign Language Institute. I hope to become an interpreter.'

'Are you staying at the hotel?'

'No, I am a native of Hainan Island. Hainan Island is the second largest island in China.'

'Oh? What is the largest?'

'Taiwan!' (The Chinese persist in believing Taiwan to be a part of China in the hope that what they believe to be true will eventually come true.)

But we had interrupted his flow. His eyes fixed on the wall above our heads.

'Hainan Island is a tropical island with a wide variety of crops including coffee, tea, rubber, bananas and rice. The centre of the island is formed by the Limu Ling Mountains, the highest of which is the Five Finger Mountain and there are many beautiful beaches ideal for tourism. There is a population of five million people, and many important minerals can be found here such as iron ore, copper and titanium . . .'. Patrick and I could not resist nudging each other, but refrained from interrupting him again as he would never have been able to continue.

That over, he introduced himself. 'My name is Mo Chui Shao, and I am nineteen years old. I would like to be of assistance to you. What can I do to help you?'

'We are trying to buy bus tickets to the south of the island.'

'Ah, you wish to go to Sanya. Please come with me and we will go to the long-distance bus station.'

'But surely you have many things to do. It's very kind of you, but it would be boring for you to have to go down there with us.'

'No, I would like to help. It is a wonderful opportunity for me to practise my English.'

So off we went and soon, without any trouble, had two bus tickets for Sanya, leaving tomorrow. We were jubilant: it was our last hope of relief from the depressing weather.

'Now I would like to show you some of our beautiful sights of Haikou.'

'What sights?'

He took out a pen and wrote 'The Five Official Memorial Temper'.

'It is close to my father's house. First we can visit that, and then we can go home and have some tea and I can show you my tape recorder and my English books.'

Out in the suburbs the rain streamed off palm trees and turned paddy fields into square brown lakes. The 'temper' was a classical Chinese house dedicated to the memory of five reforming officials. The pillars were painted shiny vermilion and Chui Shao said it had once been the home of a famous poet. I was excited for it must have been the home of Su Dongpo who after making a wrong political move was exiled to Hainan. I was sure he was one of the five reformers, for in his capacity as a Confucian scholar-official he had drained the great west lake in Hangzhou, and as a poet he wrote not only of nature – inspiring the 'southern school' of landscape painting – but also of poverty and suffering. I imagined him in his silken robes (on finer days than this) strolling from courtyard to courtyard through rooms without doors leading out to his bamboos and his magnolias and his rock garden.

Classical Chinese houses do not separate interior and exterior spaces as houses do in the West. In China a garden is often enclosed by buildings to become part of the house, and the house is open and filled with plants to become part of the garden. Like so many beautiful places, it had been vandalised during the Cultural Revolution and was now being restored.

'Now we will go and have some tea. Please follow me.' Considering Chui Shao's educated manner and expensive-looking clothes, his home came as a shock. It was in a dismal multi-storey block surrounded by the ubiquitous dirty new cars. We climbed the oozing concrete steps to the fifth floor and walked down an open corridor through the horizontal rain which swept in from across the flooded fields, to the last door on the left. Inside was a cramped room lit by a bare light bulb and furnished with two narrow bunk beds, a wooden bench and a small desk at which, Chui Shao proudly explained, he did all his English studies. He shared this room with his father.

He must have seen our dismay, for he hastened to reassure us. 'This is not our real home,' he said. 'This is just the headquarters of my father's company, the Qiongshan County Foodstuffs Corporation. We live here because I have been attending Haikou Middle and Senior schools, and because my father works here.'

'Where is your real home?'

'Our real home is in the country, a long way away, about twenty-five kilometres. That is where my mother and three younger brothers live, in a big new house. I visit them for a few days every six months. I have just returned from there in fact, after the New Year holiday. But look! Here is my father coming now. He will be very happy to meet you.'

Chui Shao's father, though he spoke no English, was friend-ly and welcoming. The boys living next door and the young manager of the company all came to meet us, and soon biscuits and sweet black tea were provided. Mr Mo senior sat up on his bunk swinging his legs and smiling.

Chui Shao – or 'Little Mo' as he liked to be called – showed us his English-Chinese dictionaries from Oxford University Press, his notebooks diligently filled with vocabulary, trans-lations and grammar, and his copies of the *China Daily*, the English language newspaper. These he wanted me to have, even though they were obviously very precious to him with words he did not understand carefully underlined and translated. I had to force him to accept my refusal.

'My father says he is very sorry that we do not have dinner ready for you, but of course he did not know you were coming.'

We laughed. 'Perhaps you would like to come and have dinner with us?'

'Oh no, I couldn't, not at the Overseas Chinese Hotel.' He was intimidated by its grandeur.

'All right, we won't go there. You can choose the place.'

'Do you mean you want to eat a simple meal of rice?'

'Of course. Let's go.'

We said goodbye to Mr Mo and all the other residents of the building, and took the bus back to Haikou. Though Chui Shao was initially shy about eating with us, he soon relaxed and we three became friends. We parted late, waving him off on his bus back home.

'Don't forget to telephone me when you return to Haikou,' he called. 'I am going to cook dinner for you!'

It was a pity we were leaving the next day – we would have liked to spend more time with him, and we both looked forward to seeing him again.

– 4 –

Sanya and Baoting: the countryside

Sanya: junks shaped like galleons under fluttering red flags; a girl with long stiff plaits stands to row herself ashore, where shacks sink on stilts into mud. Over the bridge come old peasant women in baggy black trousers and black shirts tied across the neck, swaying on bare feet, tough and splayed, under shoulder poles and baskets of vegetables. Beneath stocky palm trees stand rows of taxis – ancient motor bikes with side-cars – drivers with feet up and hats down waiting for a fare; and huddles of Li minority girls in blue scarves and straw hats chew betel and laugh together, and try to sell the watches strapped up their arms to the sailors who saunter by and flirt.

Out into the high street seeps the smell of fish, and, in the market, shoppers haggle over weird-looking catches. Women with babies strapped to their backs squat over mounds of tea and ginger weighed out on tiny scales, and down at the end, hidden behind a wall, men gamble illegally. Beyond is the beach where women come to wash out fishy baskets and a small boy in a PLA cap comes to play and to talk to himself. Moored close by is a fishing boat: we take photographs and two fishermen wave.

The smell of fish is getting stronger, for here is the harbour where rusted ships tie up along the quay and women spread thousands of sprats out on the ground to dry, glistening in the stormy light like pearly shells, the bad ones picked out with chopsticks.

Along the coast rough prickly dunes give way to sand, warm

and unwashed, and beyond to the steep cream beach and the sea. Sun at last! As we had crossed the Limu Ling mountains, so the sun had gleamed with a lemony light through the clouds.

We walked down the beach, away from a group of Chinese boys jumping in the waves, and tentatively I took off a layer of clothes. The warm air on my skin was delicious. We lay on the sand and swam and I collected shells, my eyes on the tideline but my thoughts miles and miles away over the South China Sea to Thailand and to memories of Christmas on another island, and further away to other beaches, to other days collecting shells, to other people who collected shells – my mother, my sisters, my grandmother. But then I looked up and remembered that I was here, in China, now, on a coral beach shadowed by palm trees under the deep saturated blue light before a storm and I gloried in it, and in the succession of chances that had brought me here.

Another late afternoon and the sun swelled up into an orange bag and collapsed into the sea. The sea whispered but was hardly able to ripple on to the shore. I lay half awake, dreamily moving my feet through the corally sand, feeling out the shells, breathing the hot pine scent that hovered in the still dusk air. What did I dream? Perhaps of the legendary Ah Kei, who chased a deer from Five Finger Mountain over ninety-nine mountains and ninety-nine rivers, unable to capture it until he reached this very spot where I now lay. Here his prey could run no further, for it was trapped by the ocean, and Ah Kei at last raised his bow and arrow and took aim. But as he was about to shoot, the deer turned its head, and gazed at Ah Kei. He paused, and to his astonishment saw the deer becoming a mountain, and out of the mountain walking a beautiful girl. She, a spirit, had fallen in love with this young and bold huntsman, and the local Li people are their descendants . . . That explains why there is a hotel here called *Luhuitou*, the Hotel of the Deer turns its Head . . . I slept.

Suddenly a motorbike roared up and a boy shouted from the pine woods. He ran past us, pulling off his clothes and yelling,

and charged into the sea. He seemed to multiply as more boys
arrived, running down the beach from every side, arms rotating, calling us to join them. A dark shadow moved across the
bay just under the surface of the water – a submarine? A whale?
Then it exploded, water arching up into the sky, cliffs booming, the boys jumping and laughing and splashing about. Fish
came floating to the surface and were stuffed into nets, into
mouths, into anything that would hold more. Patrick joined
them; a little dumb girl sat beside me on the beach and
gestured her excitement when the shoal was brought in.

Grinning at us, a man mimed eating so off we went together
to a small outdoor café near the beach where we agreed on a
price with the cook and soon ate fresh fish sitting under the
palm trees and the full moon and the stars in the warm night.
With a mixture of sign language, our phrase book, and bottles
of Chinese beer, we managed to communicate, mostly to tell
each other that the fish was *hao* (good), that the place was *hao*,
that we were all feeling *hao*. Patrick pushed his straw hat to the
back of his head and looked like Little Boy Blue and he and the
fisherman smoked each other's cigarettes. Some men squatting beneath the trees around a lamp called us over to join
them, and we talked about the moon, and man walking on the
moon. Then we climbed into our friend's side-car to be driven
back along the deserted coastal path, the sea beside us black
and still.

I raised my cup to drink to the guests; and we chanted the
full moon ode, and sang out the verse about the modest lady.
After a while the moon came up between the dipper and the
herdboy star; a dewy whiteness spanned the river, merging
the light on the water into the sky. We let the tiny reed drift
on its course, over ten thousand acres of dissolving surface
which streamed to the horizon, as though we were leaning
on the void with the winds for chariot.

[Su Dongpo, *The Red Cliff*]

We helped the old ferry women to row us across the harbour.
The town was dark now except in the brightly-lit snooker sheds
where boys hover like moths until late at night practising their
shots.

'Why don't we play?' suggested Patrick.

'All right.'

We should have known. Within seconds everyone had
abandoned their own game for ours, clustering round us five or
six people deep. I felt nervous: I had never played before and
no one smiled indulgently at my first feeble attempts. The
atmosphere was not the light-hearted one of the fishermen.

'I don't want to play any more. One of you can take my cue.' I
offered it around but they all shied away. Then one boy
stepped forward and snatched it; without a word or a smile he
began the game and the crowd closed in again. The Chinese
against the foreigner: what could be better? Amongst the crush
of bodies and under the bare white bulb both the boy and
Patrick began to sweat. I could not watch any more, and forced
my way back out of the crowd to lean against a table near the
cool entrance. This boy was so serious, determined to win. I
willed Patrick not to shame us, but I couldn't bear to look.
Patrick won the first game, and the boy looked angry. Then the
boy won the second game and he looked triumphant. It was
over: one game each. The boy shook Patrick curtly by the hand
and stalked off followed by a troupe of smaller boys. We left,
alone.

As we crossed the bridge, a cyclist called out gaily in English,
'Hello, goodnight.' It was the boy.

We left the coast and ventured up into the mountains above
lakes and steep forests to the prosperous but dull Tongshe,
capital of the Hainan Autonomous Region, and then on to
Baoting. Opposite the bus station a dusty hallway filled with
iron beds was the *lushe*, a lodging reserved for Chinese only, so
we were led to the *zhaodaisuo* which was reserved for government officials. It was like a large country house, overlooking the
village and dropping levels of fish ponds. There was no one

about. Hesitantly we called out *Ni Hao*, hello, and a door banged. Footsteps approached from the other end of the building. It was a woman in a dark-blue suit, her hair tied back in two bunches. She looked amazed to see us. We tried to explain, and another girl appeared, this one in bright pink jeans and a matching pink jacket, obviously from Hong Kong.

'Do you speak Mandarin?' she inquired helpfully in a high pitched voice.

'No, not very well.'

'I will help you then. My name is Florence. I am here with my family, though we are not staying, just passing through.'

'Where are your family?'

'They are just finishing dinner. Excuse me please, I must return to them in a moment as we are leaving soon, but first I will help you settle in.'

We did not worry that someone would occupy one of the other three beds in our spacious room, as every other room in the hotel was empty. Even so, each day the woman in the blue suit refilled every thermos and dusted every mosquito net and plastic slipper, doing her job just in case.

There was a restaurant beside the hotel, another huge and empty building, but we were too late for dinner, and it had to be ordered in advance so we turned to go. Just then Florence reappeared.

'Please join us,' she said. 'My family and the Baoting leaders would be very honoured.'

Ignoring our protests – we did not want to intrude and were both so scruffy – she opened the door to a private room where ranged around a large table were Florence's family, the head of Baoting and a select group of cadres. They rose to greet us, shaking hands all round, and though they had finished eating insisted that we joined them and found us chairs, bowls, and chopsticks. It was a huge and lavish banquet with untouched dishes of every sort of delicious and exotic food and bowls of a strong rice wine like an alcoholic rice pudding.

'Please eat,' they urged, selecting the best morsels for us and politely picking at a few things themselves to keep us company. It was all so sudden and so grand that we both felt overwhelmed by their hospitality. Glasses were raised and we were toasted *Ganbei* as the first foreigners to have eaten here. We, already flushed, replied with our toasts to them, to Baoting, to Hainan, to the future!

Florence's uncle was planning to invest in tourism on the island, and this was the reason for the banquet. Hainan was his home before he and his family escaped from poverty to Canton, and then from the Cultural Revolution to Hong Kong; business men like him, investing in their homelands, are the hope of all developing areas of China. Florence's father was a painter who exported his works to the USA; he was clearly a little bored by the business deals, and seizing Patrick's camera climbed artistically on to the windowsill to take photo after photo of us all.

Then, as suddenly as it started, the banquet was over. It is considered good manners to leave some food uneaten, even though most Chinese never see such delicacies as these. Florence and her family disappeared in their hired car, and we were whisked off for a tour of the town. Couples strolled under plane trees, pausing to buy sticks of sugar cane, slices of watermelon, newspaper cones of melon seeds. Others looked through heaps of multi-coloured plastic shoes, or crowded outside the cinemas: those who cannot afford to see the film can at least listen as it is broadcast outside on loudspeakers. It was Friday night and there were fireflies in the air.

The next morning we set off into the country, walking first through a collection of buildings like a barracks behind a forbidding gate. There were people shopping at a stall and others repairing a tractor; children shouted from a playground outside a school. I thought again of the Hmong refugee camp in Thailand. But this was not a prison or a camp, this was a commune or its subdivision of a *Danwei* (work unit). Communes, work units – they seemed so far from the world of cadres entertaining Hong Kong businessmen, things from an era already past. Yet of all the recent changes, the most dramatic have been here amongst the peasants. Since it was admitted that the vast collectives had been a failure, the fields have been returned to individual farmers. In this new 'Responsibility System', families or individuals care for a particular piece of land; though it varies from unit to unit, on the whole a certain amount of their produce still goes to the government but the rest is now theirs to do with as they please – to keep, to sell to the state, or to sell in the free markets that have sprung up.

We left the buildings for groves of rubber trees that spread their yellow-green branches over small hills. Like beech trees they have no undergrowth, just last autumn's dry brown leaves. Along a pink-earthed track we came upon a hamlet of mud-walled, straw-roofed cottages out of which faces peered, and then darted away. Three small boys watched startled from their fire on the hillside, the air so still that the smoke hung motionless around them, framing them. From far away came the chink of iron on stone as someone worked in a quarry. Nestling below us were revealed the narrow secret valleys, the lush smooth green of the paddy fields broken only by the yellow disc of a straw hat and the blue back of a worker as she bent to weed between the shoots, singing to herself. A fat blotched pig trailing piglets scuffled out from the woods, and disappeared; mosquitoes hovered, and a chameleon on a stalk blinked its bulging eyes.

Past tattered banana plants and giant ferns we rested by a river and bathed our feet and watched an old woman in a tall conical hat lead her two buffaloes in and out of the water, up the bank, down into the stream, talking to them all the time. She hardly saw us, so absorbed was she in her buffalo world.

Our next destination was Wanning, chosen simply because it was the closest place on the map. We had a few hours to wait for the bus, so we sat in a teahouse nearby. It was as squalid as most Hainan cafés, with round tables swinging on broken stone stumps, covered in greasy fly-ridden cloths, the floor thick and sticky with grime. Patrick went off to take photographs while I sat in a corner to write my diary in peace. I was deeply involved in my flow of intimate confidences when I felt someone standing at my elbow and realised a man was watching me write. It made me uneasy and after a brief smile I tried to ignore him. But he was joined by another man, and another until I sat back and looked around me at a crowd of fifty or more. The message had spread as it does from bee to bee. As one man moved away so he was replaced by another, all jostling to get a closer look. I carried on writing, and they hemmed in tighter. I began to panic. My only escape was through the windows but these were now blocked by a wall of children, children on each other's shoulders, clinging to the bars, more eyes peering over the sill. They gazed at me through the bars as if I was a creature in a zoo; it was funny and bizarre and so unnerving that I had to say something to defuse the situation. 'Can you read it?' I asked. I knew they could not, but I wanted to make sure. They stared back uncomprehending, not speaking, not smiling, just staring, at me and at the unknown twirls and loops that struggled across my page. Could this happen to a Chinese girl in a remote village in England, I wondered? I doubt it. I felt exposed and trapped.

'Come back Patrick,' I urged silently, and when he did, the crowd evaporated at once. What would happen when there was no Patrick to return? I did not want to think about it.

Gui Gian and the Lantern Festival

A dapper young man wearing a grey suit and a tie pin leant out of the bus to say farewell, again, to a sophisticated girl. He was proud of her and explained to us over the heads of other passengers, 'That my girl friend.' She smiled indulgently and waved him off. He had an endearing face with wiry hair that stuck up almost at the same angle as his bright slanting eyes, and an ingenuous, charming smile; I liked him at once. By way of an introduction he sent oranges and cigarettes down the bus to us and shouted that his name was Ying Gui Gian and he was home on holiday from the navy in Shanghai.

'Where you go?' he shouted.

'Wanning.'

'Oh good! Tonight you is welcome to our family.'

'What did he say?' whispered Patrick.

'I don't know. Something about his family.'

Wanning was disappointing. The brick houses were dilapidated and interspersed with even scruffier cafés, and recent attempts to smarten it up with road widenings and the inevitably ugly new buildings had only made it all the more drab.

'Tonight you is welcome to our family,' said Gui Gian again.

I felt weary: even allowing for the charm of Gui Gian, an hour in Wanning, I said to myself, is an hour too long.

He took us to the 'hotel' and it was one of the worst I had seen. A small room like an attic high up on the top floor provided two camp beds shrouded in mosquito nets heavy with dust. I brushed against one, and the dust rose, hovered for a while, and then sank back down again. Only a few panes of jagged glass remained in the window, and there was only one light switch to serve all five rooms on this floor. Down below some boys washed clothes at a well, and a pig grunted. Behind a low wall I thought I had intruded on its sty but no, this was the *cesuo*, the loo – an open sewer. The Chinese families that appeared to live in this hotel had abandoned it, preferring the flat roof outside our door.

'This very good?' Gui Gian smiled.

'Yes, it's fine.'

Gui Gian was clearly in his element organising our accommodation, fixing the price with the manager (about twenty pence) and marching us through the town to his family.

'Tonight streets very well,' he enthused. What could he mean?

The town opened out into paddy fields surrounded by a new development of smart brick bungalows with upturned eaves and tiled Chinese landscapes decorating the windows. Gui Gian strode through a courtyard, greeting friends as he passed, to the last of the houses set on its own under palm trees.

'This my home,' he said. 'Sit down please.'

Folding metal chairs were taken from a stack against the wall and opened round a low table in the centre of the room. It was sparsely furnished and the floor was bare stone, but it was cheerful, the walls decorated with posters of classical landscapes (without figures) and calligraphy, and a large black and white portrait of Gui Gian's mother. Propped against a mirror was a colour snapshot of Gui Gian himself standing in his sailor's uniform beside a bridge in Nanjing. A cabinet at the far end of the room was filled with trinkets, and there was an altar on which incense burned to the household gods. It was so different from Mr Xie's comfortless flat in Canton. As an 'Autonomous Region' and an island, Hainan is far more relaxed than the mainland.

Once again, it was as though telepathy had spread the message, and we were instantly at the centre of a circle of

– 59 –

family, friends, neighbours, children, all crowding into the room, setting out the rest of the metal chairs and sitting in rows like an audience in a village hall. Boys were peering through the windows and whispering; one would blurt out 'Hello' or 'Bye bye', and they all giggled.

First Gui Gian's mother was brought forward to meet us. She was a beautiful, elegant, shy person, dressed in traditional black trousers, her long grey hair tied in two plaits wrapped neatly round her head. Gui Gian's brother ran a restaurant in Baoting, his uncle worked for the local post office, and we met more brothers and more uncles – all the younger men were introduced as brothers and all the older men as uncles, and there were several girls who were 'girl friends'. Gui Gian's younger sister greeted us coolly and left the room. Perhaps she resented our intrusion. But minutes later she reappeared, transformed, in high-heeled shoes, flared jeans and a fancy red waistcoat, hair swept up elaborately on top, specially for us.

As for me, I had had my hair clipped and razored in Thailand. It was cool and liberating but now was causing some confusion. 'They think you is boy,' Gui Gian confided, and sniggered.

Glasses of tea were produced, and Gui Gian opened a bag of sweets which he emptied into a bowl.

'Please, heylp yoorsell, have more tea.' He was most assiduous, replenishing our glasses after almost every sip. His sister-in-law arrived from next door with plates of dried fish and square cubes of pork fat, and she ladled out bowls of rice gruel from a rice boiler.

'Heylp yoorsell,' urged Gui Gian.

'But isn't this your family's supper, that they were about to have?'

He dismissed the idea. 'They eat already.'

It was difficult to eat the repulsive fat, and especially in front of such a large audience. Gui Gian misinterpreted our unease and signalled to his sister whereupon two spoons were brought.

'No it's all right,' said Patrick. 'We prefer the chopsticks.'

There was silence, and Gui Gian shook his head.

'Food very bad,' he said.

'No, no, it's delicious.'

He looked at his watch and was suddenly in a hurry.

'We go now. Follow me please.'

There was hardly time to say goodbye before we were following him back to the town, and the little boys had scampered off laughing into the dark. Gui Gian seemed agitated.

'Where are we going?' Patrick whispered.

'Back to our hotel I suppose.'

'Why is he walking so fast?'

'Perhaps he has many things to do.'

He was hurrying, faster and faster; we could hardly keep up. Out from a schoolroom came the sound of someone practising a drum roll. Something was building up, but what? A child with its face covered in pink make-up was following us. I heard shouting, and a green firework flew up. We turned a corner to see the streets had exploded into life: the squalid town had been transformed into an enchanted world. Under multi-coloured bunting were now hundreds – thousands – of people swarming round candle-lit tables, buying oranges and sugar cane, buying bowls of tea. There were children in PLA caps held high on the shoulders of excited fathers, and ancient men and women whose eyes gleamed out of tortoise-wrinkled faces. There were little girls in party ribbons, older girls in new trouser suits, all milling together.

A rhythmic drum beat approached. Runners forced the crowd back against the walls and between them marched men in blue track suits pounding a deep bass drum on a sedan chair under a canopy, and clashing cymbals. Behind came a green and gold paper dragon hundreds of feet long, supported by thirty men clutching poles in gloved hands. They lurched this way and that as the dragon swerved and reared its head at a sparkly pole twirled in front, tormenting it. The dragon paused and spread itself out horizontally across the street, the drum beat quickening, then head and tail charged forward together as the firecrackers crackled and spectators cheered.

More dragons followed, an orange and gold one, smaller green ones, miniature ones carried by children, lions with round hairy faces and shaggy bodies. Behind came processions of crazy people on stilts, eight or nine feet tall, with white and pink painted faces, others dressed as grey-coated monks in tall pointed caps like wimples, and devils in skull masks dancing about to tease the crowd, sending the smallest children screaming to their parents, the braver children taunting the devils back. I remembered how excited we had tried to be by the pathetic procession in Zhanjiang and laughed out loud, but even tonight's display was but a practice run for the festivities we were to see over the next few days. Quite by chance we had arrived in time for the Lantern Festival, celebrated during the full moon fifteen days after New Year, and one of the most fabulous occasions in China.

Through it all our friend cleared a path for us shouting, 'Follow me please! Where is Helena?'

'I'm here, behind you.'

'Aren't you called Patrick?'

'No, he's Patrick.'

We ran upstairs into a restaurant to see the revelry from above, then down again, Gui Gian ordering people to move aside so that we could take photographs, while we begged him not to trouble himself on our behalf. But the men carrying the dragons seemed pleased and even staged elaborate coils and turns for us.

'This very bad,' Gui Gian yelled over the noise. 'Tomorrow streets very well.' This, it seemed, was just a practice run. Many people stopped to greet our friend – it was a long time since he had last been home – and he introduced them as uncles or brothers or 'school mats'. They were curious and friendly, and we all shook hands when we met and then immediately again as we parted. One man came from Baoting.

'He say he saw you there,' Gui Gian told us.

The rest of the throng was amazed to see foreigners in their midst. Many had come in to Wanning from remote villages so had never seen TV, let alone a real live foreigner, and they would turn to watch the dragon, notice us, and the dragon would be forgotten. They gaped at us and nudged their friends, and we could watch the astonishment spread. Hundreds of people gathered round, and stared and stared. I felt like a celebrity and also like a curio – a giant or an elephant woman on show in a circus. I would shout 'Hello' or wave, but they did not know how to react to this peculiar monster and expressions of horror, fear and mirth surrounded me. Much to Gui Gian's amusement, the main topic under discussion was whether or not I was a boy. They decided I was, and I enjoyed my new role: I felt a new boldness as I stared back at them all. Many were as fascinating to me as I was to them, particularly the Hmong women in short embroidered skirts, purple, blue and pink, and matching embroidered leggings and scarves. I also enjoyed the feeling that by being passively observed, I was in a way actively participating, for here before them was their first ever view of a 'foreign guest'. The crowd was not aggressive, but sometimes grew claustrophobically large, and Gui Gian, seeing my look of desperation, would shout something and they smiled or looked ashamed, and temporarily dispersed, parting the crowd for us to walk away. But as soon as we stopped walking they closed in again.

At last the processions ended and we parted for the night, shaking hands warmly. 'I see you tomorrow morning,' Gui Gian promised eagerly. 'Six o'clock all right?'

'Perhaps a little later.'

He was knocking on our door by eight o'clock, still very smart in his grey suit and tie pin, if a little crumpled. Perhaps in all the excitement he had not been to bed. With him was his seven-year-old nephew, dressed in little flared trousers decorated with appliqué cartoon characters.

'We go Dongsangfar! Dongsangfar very well,' Gui Gian announced, his eyebrows going up and down, his eyes bright. We had no idea what Dongsangfar was, but followed him towards what we thought was a bus station. It was a grand building set amongst well tended trees and box hedges, and we were led into a room with a map of Wanning on the wall. I saw we were close to the sea, and wondered if Dongsangfar was a beach. 'Sit down please.' This was obviously not a bus station, it was too grand, but we did not know what else it could be. A succession of men were brought to meet us, and they were introduced either as 'My friend,' or as 'Wanning County Officer.' Perhaps we were in the local government buildings.

Again there was much shaking of hands. Gui Gian seemed to be asking for something, or making some kind of deal; everyone we met was offered cigarettes, and even if the person was smoking already it was accepted and stuck in a top pocket for later. Sometimes they argued, 'Have one of mine, no please, have one of mine.' Every now and then Patrick would have to accept one for good form's sake – women on the other hand are expected not to smoke. It was fascinating to watch this ritual over the next few days: whenever someone wanted anything, a cigarette was offered in open and unsubtle bribery. Now Gui Gian was asking favours; later we saw a younger boy greet him and offer him a cigarette, and Gui Gian grandly refused.

A smiling man who walked around with his cigarette packet permanently thrust open to everyone was introduced as a 'Leader' rather than just an 'Officer'. He had the florid face and rough coarse hands of a farmer, and he was friendly. He took us across the gardens to another building where a door was unlocked into a musty room that smelled like a church, with two long green sofas covered in white antimacassars facing each other over a low table. The windows were flung open and dust blown off the plastic flowers.

'Sit down please.'

Tea was brought, and another Wanning County 'Leader'

The single child per family is the most treasured member of society.

继续大力抓紧抓好计划生育工作

Discouraging the traditional preference for male babies, 'One child, One family' posters always show a healthy girl.

Friendly faces.

Since 1983 thousands of criminals have been executed; public notice-boards serve as warnings to others.

Pig in a basket,
Hainan Island

Hmong (Miao) minority women, Sanya.

Irrigation: despite much-trumpeted reforms, rural life remains bound by ceaseless toil . . .

. . . though work is harder for some than for others.

P.L.A. soldiers on a day trip.

Street medicine: free entertainment for passers-by.

Buddhist monk.

came to meet us. He seemed superior to the others, dressed austerely in a cool blue Mao suit buttoned up to the neck. He was very different from his simple rough colleague, with soft fat hands and a limp handshake, and a smooth, soft voice. Gui Gian introduced him deferentially as '*The* Wanning County Leader', and I wondered what he had done during the Cultural Revolution; he looked sinister and shrewd.

'Wanning County Leader say, Welcome to Wanning.'

'Thank you. Please tell him we are very pleased to be here.'

We sipped our tea. 'Heylp yoorsell,' said Gui Gian. His nephew stood in a corner poking his finger into the electric fan. Gui Gian and the leader seemed to be arguing. The leader looked angry, and Gui Gian harassed.

'Wanning Leader say, People's Hotel no good. You go Dongsangfar,' and he smiled his charming smile that clearly no one could resist. So Dongsangfar was not a beach.

A new Mitsubishi minibus drove up, and Gui Gian said it was for us. This was what I had dreaded: perhaps Gui Gian had hired it and we, the rich foreigners, would have to pay. But no, we were to be taken on a tour of the local beauty spots, courtesy of the Wanning County Officers.

'Dongsangfar very well,' Gui Gian said again.

Sitting in the mini-bus as it hooted and pushed apart the crowds, we felt very dignified, but also like charlatans. We were being welcomed as VIPs, but had no trade deals to offer, no investments in tourism: we were just two innocent travellers who had come to Wanning by chance, in our silly peasant straw hats and dirty jeans. Did they realise how insignificant we were? They must have done.

Our destination turned out to be a smart old hotel on a rocky hillside: it was here that the officials wanted us to stay. 'This Dongsangfar,' said Gui Gian.

'But we want to be in the town, where everything is happening. We don't want to be stuck away up here.' We insisted, and reluctantly the officials agreed that we could stay in the town as long as we moved to a better hotel. They did not want us out of the way: they were genuinely (and rightly) ashamed of the doss house we had stayed in, but they were baffled by our refusal to come up to this beautiful place, of which they were evidently very proud.

We filed up little stone paths past a pavilion to an outcrop of large rocks inscribed with red Chinese characters which Gui Gian said were pieces of poetry about the loveliness of the landscape. Far away below us was a wide flat valley divided neatly into rectangular strips of paddy, the only vertical features a ruined pagoda standing alone on its mound, and clumps of palm trees. The rocks were sacred, and in a cave was a temple. A long-bearded deity lurked behind an altar, and around it people jostled, pushing forward one of the family who knelt down and shook a stick out of a box. This stick had a symbolic number wrapped around it which was interpreted by an old wise man. Outside was another man with a pink sheet covered in stylised faces from which he read people's fortunes, and another had pictures of hands. Since neolithic times this ancient art of divination has been practised in China; it is detailed in the *I Ching*, the Book of Change, one of the most ancient of the Chinese classics. Chinese religion interweaves the 'three teachings' with ancient local beliefs, animism and magic, a pantheon of deities impossible to unravel, and worshipped here, miles from any tourist centre. At Dongsangfar there was also the most ancient Chinese religion of ancestor worship, and hummocking the hillside were recognisable mounds of earth like big molehills that are the graves.

'That my father.' Gui Gian pointed out one particular swelling in the distance. Along the edges of fields, beside railway tracks, there is always a small piece of land set aside for the ancestors. If the ancestors are cared for and respected, they in turn will protect their descendants.

Dongsangfar was popular, and people climbed the steps and walkways over the rocks taking photos of each other posing under the red writing. They all seemed to have cameras – Chinese 'Seagull' cameras with black and white film; Gui Gian had one, and we too climbed about and posed under a poem while he smiled proudly. He revelled in being host and guide, and nothing was too much trouble: there were some slimy green caves and, despite his best suit, he was eager to crawl down inside if we wanted. He bought us all yard-long sticks of sugar cane and we stood by the road spitting out woody sugary shreds. 'Dongsangfar very well,' we all agreed.

By the time we returned to the town, the throng had swollen so much that we had to abandon the van. There were even more people than the night before, a sea of yellow straw hats, a multitude of different shapes – panamas, straws wide and flat, tall thin stove pipes, old women in black velvet berets. Streams of cyclists were arriving, often mother, father and two children all balanced on one bike (families are allowed up to four children here); others struggled along with a pig slung across the back, or a box filled with ducks, for this was not only the Lantern Festival but also a huge annual market. The streets were littered with bits of sugar cane and red shreds from the firecrackers.

'Streets very dirty,' apologised Gui Gian.

'No, they're fine.' I said.

A few minutes later he said it again, very ashamed.

'Oh,' said Patrick, 'It's only fireworks from the festival.'

We took it in turns to reassure him, he was so genuinely concerned that everything should be wonderful. We paused to watch a fight between the proprietors of two neighbouring restaurants, the owners screaming at each other, waving their arms and shaking their fists, even lunging out. A son tried to intervene and restrain his old father, but he escaped and sprang out, shouting threats over the dividing wall and shaking his fists again. Passers-by enjoyed it, cheering them on and laughing, but Gui Gian tried to hurry us away. He did not like us to see this shameful behaviour. It was the same later: we stopped beside a circle of men enthralled by something on the pavement, all crouching in a tight circle. They were gambling, winding up a toy truck and betting on its destination. 'In

China this very bad,' Gui Gian disapproved, and urged us on.

But he was particularly proud of a new restaurant that had been built along the main street, so we suggested we took him there for lunch. We were standing in the garden at Wanning County Offices when Gui Gian noticed a friend walking past, so he introduced us and offered him a cigarette; in a few minutes the minibus had reappeared to take us all to the restaurant and, behind a screen, we were entertained to another Baoting-style banquet. The waitress was introduced as a 'school mat', and when we told her how pleased we were to meet her, Gui Gian shook his head and said sorrowfully – but proudly too – 'She no spik Englis. They say I is your interpreter!' And then he laughed and laughed at this preposterous idea. But so he was. We had had the extraordinary luck to meet the only person in the entire area who spoke even a word of English. We called for the bill, but no no, Wanning County Officer pay. The restaurant manager was brought out to meet us and be congratulated on his superb food and like a royal troupe we departed with our entourage to change hotels. The new hotel was slightly less repellent with a balcony overlooking the street, and we asked how much it would be.

'Wanning County Officer pay.' Their kindness seemed unlimited: for the rest of our stay there, we never paid for anything, and dined in style in the Wanning County Officers' own dining room.

We escaped for a while to rest from the crowd. In daylight the staring was even worse than at night, and as both of us towered over the tiny people we were always spotted. 'Yingwo, Yingwo, English,' we heard passed from friend to friend. (It had seemed easier not to mention Belgium as well.) But even up on our balcony where we thought we could watch in secret we were noticed. A truck loaded with boys in maroon tracksuits drove past and one noticed us and told his friends and they all waved and smiled.

Patrick and I looked at each other and marvelled at it all.

What we had seen the night before was nothing, Gui Gian promised, to what we would see tonight. We joined the steadily swelling crowds and headed towards a main street lined with faceless municipal buildings – the police station and fire brigade – that had been touchingly decorated with lanterns and red streamers. The procession was still being prepared and Gui Gian grew agitated once more, rushing about to find good angles for photographs. Close up in the golden candle lights we could see the sophistication of the floats. Lorries were completely disguised under paper sculptures of a giant ox, a pig, an illuminated peacock with a fanning green tail, life underwater with children riding fish that were lit from within and appeared to swim, their tails and heads swung by hidden people. There was a lantern that slowly revolved, each window revealing a costumed, sleeve-dancing child. There was a girl dressed as a pearl, her arms the two shells of the oyster; there was a small child sitting quite rigid in the palm of another, held up by a hidden frame, her only movement to wave a bunch of flowers like a frothing wand. Heavily made up men enjoyed their campery, and a procession of little boys marched under paper goldfish lanterns lit by candles. One float was in the charge of a frenzied man, desperately overexcited about getting us to photograph his team, straightening this, tidying that, organising the poses, even providing us with a ladder for a better view. The batteries of my flash were dying and Gui Gian rushed off to find some more.

There were not only traditional images but modern ones too. The school float displayed a large revolving globe and nodding satellite – China taking its place in world politics. There was a relief map of Hainan studded with miniature tower blocks, an aeroplane flying over the highest point of the island, Five Finger Mountain: a budding Taiwan. There was a lorry converted into a disco in which men and women were self-consciously dancing; even the department store was there, its float lit not with candles but with blinding white neon, and instead of fabulous dragons and fish there were badly sketched

TVs, bicycles, rice cookers and fans. In a niche in the side of the lorry sat the curly-haired waitress from lunch, the 'school mat', with a display of cassette recorders and fans: a celebration of the new consumer market, the new China.

The procession was beginning. 'Follow me please, follow me,' called Gui Gian, and we pushed past a police barrier to climb on to a flat roof where some officials were drinking tea. They greeted us, and Gui Gian handed out cigarettes, and after much hand shaking we were made 'warmly welcome' and given official red ribbons to wear pinned to our chests. 'Now we Wanning County Officers!' Gui Gian crowed, and the officials looked slightly disapproving.

A man from Hainan TV had said he wanted to take our photograph, and Gui Gian was thrilled. He found everything as funny and as exciting as we did. But we had lost the man in the crowds, and met instead two girls with curly hair wearing matching beige trouser suits who were friends of Gui Gian, and they sneaked up on to the roof top with us in time for the procession to start. Despite all the formalities, it seemed hundreds of people had crept up here too and no one seemed to mind, everyone was too enthralled by the excitements below.

The music pounded, each of the multitude of floats with its own sound effects, and past trouped the procession, pausing beneath our building for a salute to the officials before moving on along its densely packed route. Everything was golden and glittering, the floats and dragons merging into a luminous haze, the fireworks pink and white and green springing up from every rooftop as far as we could see. Sitting on our balcony hours later, we could follow the procession as it wound its way through the rejoicing town, simply by watching the successive eruptions of fireworks. It would begin again the following morning and last until late at night for the next four days, and during those days more than sixty thousand people must have filled the streets of Wanning.

The two girls were both twenty-two years old and worked in a local tea plantation. One had learnt three essential words of

English, and she wrapped her arm around me and said, 'I love you.' Her friend took my other hand in her sticky little palm. In front of us, I watched Gui Gian entwining his fingers through Patrick's, and I struggled to repress my laughter. Hand in hand, the girls behind the boys, we returned to our hotel room to have a party. Gui Gian taught the girls the two-step while we drank tea and watched the last stray dragons go by again.

The next day I expressed a wish to visit the pagoda we had seen from Dongsangfar. I expected Gui Gian to show us where to catch the bus, but should have known better by now, for he was a djinn who could conjure up anything. A Toyota jeep appeared, with two officials, and we left the town in style. Again I felt uneasy as we glided past the families who work from dawn until late evening in the fields, even during the festival. A man was pumping water into the paddy fields by treading a wheel round and round all day. He was still there when we returned, slumped and exhausted. Everyone has work to do: an old man was herding ducks, boys lay on the backs of buffaloes, children looked after smaller children: one fifth of the world are Chinese peasants and for all the new economic reforms their lives are still bound by ceaseless toil.

We went first to the coast, past brick kilns and villages to rough pine trees and scrub then sand dunes which opened out to long curving beaches.

'Hainan Dao very beautiful,' Gui Gian murmured. 'You tell everyone in England about Hainan.' He smiled dreamily.

Half ironically Patrick said 'Yes, I can see it will be a good place for tourism. I can envisage the hotels ringing the bay.'

The driver had none of Gui Gian's charm. 'No money,' he snapped. It was the only English he knew.

There were beaches frilled with rows of surfing waves, others dotted with fishing boats and bamboo huts. We drove on to an army camp where a man was washing. He sauntered over and pointed to a pine wood, and we walked silently through mingled smells of pine and sea to another rougher beach at the end of a spit of land where waves crashed over the boulders.

We longed to escape from all the officials and stay there alone sleeping in the woods but we knew it was not possible. We would never be able to give them the slip now, and would never be able to leave the town later without everyone hearing about it. Camping in China is, of course, illegal.

To Gui Gian's great delight, his best friend had returned from Haikou University where he taught physics, and was at home when we called. His elder brother was a Wanning County Officer, married to a policewoman, so they lived in a small but pleasant house in the grounds of the offices. However, it was as sparsely furnished as Gui Gian's with a bare stone floor and only a piece of calligraphy (written by the brother) on the wall. The whole family was there and I could see how fond they were of Gui Gian – he was so polite and full of exuberance. He told them about us, and about the officials – our meals in the officials' dining room, watching the procession from their roof-top – and they looked from Gui Gian to us and laughed with incredulity. Unfortunately none of them spoke English, and Gui Gian struggled to translate. We did discover that an American had visited this family in 1982, but he could speak Chinese so must have been better company than us. Nevertheless, they could not have been more friendly, pressing on us food and drink. Someone had brought a bunch of bananas, and the physics teacher mistook our refusals for shyness: he assumed we had never seen bananas before and did not know how to eat them, so very tactfully he himself broke off a banana and ate it in front of us, showing us how. (Funnily enough, he ate it upside down, holding it by the stalk.)

Both brothers had physics degrees from Canton University and had had to study a little English to help with the technical terminology. They had forgotten it all but had kept their English language books which they showed us. The elder brother's book was several years old and began with the word, *'Chairman Mao will live for ever in our hearts. Chairman Hua is*

our leader. We love Chairman Hua.' A story told of the good
students 'studying Marxism hard', and going out to work in
the fields with the peasants so as to learn from them and put
their Marxist theories into practice while their teacher, Com-
rade Lu, sang them American revolutionary songs. The
younger brother had a more recent book; all the Marxism and
good deeds and earnestness had vanished to be replaced by
discussion on how to make an international phone call and how
to change money at the bank.

More lavish dinners, more evenings watching the pageant:
we decided it was time to leave before everything was over. At
the end of each day I feared that something so perfect could not
be equalled, and I wanted to escape before we were disappointed and before they grew bored with us. One morning
we told Gui Gian we were leaving but, 'Today we go see coffee
plantation!' he insisted, and his face was such a picture of
disappointment and eagerness and entreaty that we could not
resist him, and stayed.

'Where are we going?'

'Wanning County Offices.'

Patrick whispered, 'I hope this boy isn't going too far.'
Perhaps he was overdoing things – we did not know what
favour he was going to ask for now. But there was nothing we
could do, so we agreed to relax and leave everything to him and
just do as we were told. If we were overstaying our welcome, it
was too bad; not being able to speak the language made our
isolation such that we could withdraw and let events around us
take their course. In the officials' restaurant a private room was
laid for a grand lunch and Gui Gian strode towards it,
imperiously calling, 'Follow me please.' But an official refused
to let us pass – it was not laid for us – and a fierce argument took
place. The argument was clearly about us, and everyone in the
dining room sat up to listen, but again there was nothing to be
done. Gui Gian was obviously getting above himself (on our
behalf) but we had to ignore it and, quietly, with affected
unconcern, we returned to our usual table. Gui Gian was

furious when he rejoined us, his hands shaking, and from time to time he yelled insults at the official but then they gave each other cigarettes and it was over. I was thankful that there were two of us: alone, this sort of incident would be very hard to bear, and as for the staring crowds and the officials, how exhausting they would all be without someone to share them. We could retreat into our own world and laugh about everything and regenerate our energies. Now, in the dining-room we could talk to each other and pretend nothing awful was happening. Once again I pushed aside my fear of being alone and concentrated on the present.

Straight after lunch we were taken to the musty room with the green sofas to see the leaders, and more food appeared – an enormous parcel of cakes and cups of delicious sweet black coffee. This, explained the officials, was Hainan coffee, and we were going to see the plantation it came from.

'Please, heylp yoorsell,' said Gui Gian.

The smooth leader was less formidable than before, now dressed in a western suit and looking more at ease. He was very gracious, asking what we did in our countries and was so impressed to hear Patrick was a specialist in tropical agriculture that he asked him to stay and work in Wanning. He said I could teach English, and we would live up at Dongsangfar which the smooth leader clearly thought an irresistible offer. I felt quite tempted – there were certainly a lot of people desperate to learn English, and it would be fun to get to know them and discover more about their way of life – but I knew I would never stay. The draw of the next place, of moving on, was always too strong.

With the help of our phrasebook and Gui Gian, this much we had understood, but most of the time we were quite confused. The leader must have seen Chinese politicians on television, and in imitation of them he spoke directly at us in Chinese while we looked fixedly back at him, nodding intelligently and smiling, but understanding not a word. Then we all turned to our interpreter who explained, 'Wanning County

Leader say, Welcome to Wanning again!' Clearly he had not said this, but we thanked him anyway. The hilarity of that day had begun.

There was some time before we were due to leave for the coffee plantation so Gui Gian invited us back to his home; he had a friend with him and we rode off on the backs of their bicycles. It was such a relief to escape from the people and the firecrackers and the officials to this calm green haven. Gui Gian's mother was squatting outside the house quietly scraping coconuts which the sister-in-law hacked apart for us – despite our protests. 'Heylp yoorsell,' said Gui Gian, opening out the folding chairs and setting them under some trees for us to sit in peace. He dressed up in his sailor's uniform and displayed himself smart and proud and a little sheepish in the doorway.

Much to our dismay, his friend asked us to change money with him on the black market. We were not interested and Gui Gian looked embarrassed. Until then, our relationship had been free of any business, and the hospitality had been so generous and so genuine that we did not want to spoil it. We all wished the friend would go and Gui Gian managed to find a way of getting rid of him. All too soon it was time to return to the fray (Gui Gian panicking about the time) and we climbed back on to the bicycles and rode out into the main street only to find that the friend's tyre was flat. Gui Gian looked frantically around him, searching for a solution, then remembered something, disappeared into a tiny house, and came out wheeling a brand new Honda 125. He, Patrick and I all jumped on the back and roared off to Wanning County Offices, leaving the friend, looking rather disconsolate, bringing up the rear on Gui Gian's bicycle. A little while later he – by now a bit puffed – struggled up the drive, and was instructed to return the motorbike. Unlike Gui Gian he had clearly never been on a motorbike before and wobbled off dangerously into the main road, all the Officers trying to hold back their smiles. That was the last we saw of him.

Awaiting us were the two leaders, the smooth and the rough and, engines purring, two black limousines with deep soft seats protected by yellow towels. Boney M played soothingly. 'This car a chapel,' said Gui Gian, and I knew what he meant. We drove along the coast and then up into the hills where serried camellia bushes rose deep green and curved away into the distance. We were visiting the Sun River tea plantation first. Women under wide straw hats picked the fresh leaves and dropped them over their shoulders into baskets on their backs.

We met the manager and tasted samples of different black and green teas, then went on to see the processing and the new German and Chinese drying equipment. The factory was spotlessly clean and all the workers – mostly women – had bare feet because so much of the sorting work is done on the floor. (We were all waved inside in our dirty shoes.) The processing looked interesting and we longed to know more, but our dear friend was not up to the translating and we grew more and more frustrated and hysterical: was this black or green tea? Before or after shredding? What was the drying temperature? He could not tell us.

On to the coffee plantations in Xinglong along one of the most lovely roads I have ever seen. I was wondering why this road should be so perfectly kept, its grassy banks mown, its palm trees whitewashed round the base of their trunks like spats, when we turned into the drive of a new and very smart hotel. As usual we were mystified: this was clearly not a coffee plantation.

We were greeted by the dignified manager, bald and freckled, and though the season had not yet started and no one was staying, we were welcomed into a tall and many-windowed room and given another sample of delicious Hainan coffee. The room was elegant, with deep armchairs draped in dust sheets, and it overlooked a verdant tropical garden growing jackfruit and a coco tree (but still no coffee in sight). The Wanning leaders were as impressed as we were, and became rather subdued. They all spoke slowly, politely, and the manager graciously addressed a few words to us, but poor Gui Gian was even more out of his depth than ever. He was nervous and giggling, sitting on the edge of his chair running his hand through his wiry hair.

'He say, Welcome to Hainan!'

'Thank you so much. Could you ask the manager . . .'

'I see, I see.'

'No, listen. Could you ask the manager who stays . . .'

'Yes I see, I see.'

'No you *don't* see.' It was becoming hilarious.

'Sorry. Manager, he say, Welcome to Hainan again!'

'Thanks. But what did he say . . .'

'Ah, I see, one moment. He say, Welcome to Hainan again, and again!'

Oh God!

The driver had sat himself in the largest and deepest of the armchairs and was now with great concentration removing his shoes. Patrick said loudly, 'Awful smell coming from this boy,' and suddenly the giggles that had been suppressed for days, waiting for a moment to erupt, came bursting out, spluttering over the coffee pretending to be coughs. Patrick fled with Gui Gian leaving me alone with the Chinese officials. I sat, and giggled. I could not stop. Think of sadness! Think of death! All I could think of were Patrick's words . . .

I found an excuse to leave the room, and splashed water on my face and tried to recover before facing them again. It was awkward, but the officials were polite and pretended nothing had happened, and we set off on a tour of the hotel. First to the hallowed rooms where the Chinese leaders stay: heavy wooden doors opened to reveal a suite of dark high rooms through which we slid on the deep red carpet. There were conference rooms and another room occupied by a vast throne-like bed beneath which nestled small black velvet slippers embroidered with a gold crest. We all felt the mattress in turn, and a look of childlike awe spread over the face of the smooth leader. The bathroom was wide and cold with an uncomfortable-looking bath, flat and square, into which pumped the hot spring for which this hotel was built.

That was the severity of 1971; now, in the new development not yet opened, things were very different. Designed by a Japanese architect, there were detached bungalows with split level interiors, Chinese lacquerware, a large music system built into the modern well-sprung bed, all financed by Overseas Chinese development investment. Here the carpets were beige: no more political red. There was a new swimming pool (in which some Chinese boys were – typically – shampooing their hair) and a terrace carpeted with fake grass on which stood plastic white tables under umbrellas advertising Marlboro. The new dining room was built on stilts over the hot spring, and from here the Chinese leaders could look out to the peasants in the fields, but through the darkened glass the peasants would be unable to see them. Behind, in a tank, was the hot spring itself. People had thrown in money, and their spirit worship seemed an incongruous but heartening sight in this sophisticated setting. A row of trees was pointed out. They looked quite uninteresting until I realised that these were the fabled coffee trees. The beans were high and unripe. We returned to the dining-room for yet another banquet.

We and the leaders all felt like children who had surprised on some magical place; even the smooth leader who grandly refused the crab, saying he ate it all the time at home, had wide excited eyes, and Gui Gian had relaxed and started to enjoy himself. As for us, *habitués* of the cheapest cafés, of bus stations and seedy hotels, we were trespassing on hallowed ground. For months and months – for as long as I could remember – we had ventured into places such as this only to slip illicitly into the pool when it was dark, or to eat the peanuts at the bar, and a feeling of conspiracy sprang up between us all and we became friends. The smooth leader was no longer sinister but charming, the rough leader was not rough but jolly, and Gui Gian entertained us all.

At a neighbouring table sat a group of politicians, including the ex-leader of Hainan austerely dressed with his Mao suit buttoned stiffly up to the neck, a member of the old guard. In front of them, and without hesitating, Gui Gian announced to the Wanning leaders that I had a Sony walkman and insisted I brought it out. They all admired it, put on one headphone each, and sat close together to listen, a look of dreamy contentment spreading over their faces. It was a wonderful sight: us in our jeans and peasant straw hats, the officials plugged into the walkman, and the old Chinese politicians, veterans of the Cultural Revolution, looking on. I wondered what they were thinking of us and our Japanese toy: less than ten years ago they would have despised us as bourgeois reactionaries, as Capitalist Roaders.

We were presented with packets of fresh coffee and sped back to Wanning as the moon rose over the sea. In the back of the car Gui Gian talked and talked, his bright eyes flashing. As we parted outside our hotel, he fought physically to refuse the gift of some coffee. He genuinely wanted nothing from our visit except that we should enjoy ourselves and tell our friends to go to Hainan too.

It was a warm still night, and alone now we wandered down a side street to find ourselves in another different but equally magical world, everything peaceful and glowing. Outside each house hung lanterns shaped as dragons and other mythical beasts revolving in the heat of the candles inside. The most exquisite was a paper eagle about to pounce on its prey, and as we paused to admire it, so its owner stood by us, pleased. But we wanted to stay anonymous tonight and not be stared at or intrude, so we slipped away. Around each door were posters saying *Gung Hay Fat Choy*, 'wishing you prosperity', and pictures of the fiendish Door God with his long black beard, fending off evil spirits. Most people were outside, sitting together in front of their houses and gossiping or watching the children play. One family sat contentedly on stools on the dusty track while inside, flat out on the floor of their front room, lay two slumbering pigs. Other families were gathered in the dark around a flickering TV set. One man watched American football, and though he invited us to join him, we shook our heads and stayed outside in the dark. It must be an extraordinary thought for those footballers that their game is watched even in an obscure town in a small island in the South China Sea. The glow of candle-light, gold and warm, was also the glow of happiness and anticipation: the familiar drum beat approached and round the corner came the dragons for the last time.

The next day we really were leaving, and though Gui Gian expressed polite sorrow, he did not argue. He looked weary, his grey suit now crumpled and rather dirty. We were late for our bus and in the heat and crush had to seek out the right one, our packs bursting with packets of tea and strong smelling coffee. After our days of luxury we were not used to fighting for public transport, and who should appear in this unsuitable setting but the two leaders to say goodbye. Gui Gian had secretly telephoned to let them know what time our bus left. They had both removed their jackets and were now sweating, buffeted by the crowd and looking flushed. We shook hands many times, promising to return, and the smooth leader apologised for not providing us with a car to take us back to Haikou; next time he said. We climbed into a bus even more rusted and decrepit than usual, and were settling in with the chickens and melon seeds and canvas sacks when Gui Gian's face (hair springing up, eyes laughing) was thrust through the window: he had found a ladder and come to say goodbye for the last time. The leaders called up to him from below.

'What did they say?'

'Wanning Leaders say, Welcome to Hainan again!'

– 6 –

Mo Chui Shao

In just two hours we were back in Haikou among the Friendship stores and Hong Kong goods, and back in the Overseas Chinese Hotel arguing with the receptionists over whether the empty beds in the dormitory were, or were not, available. It felt like months that we had been away, but so quickly the enchantment was over and we were ordinary travellers once more, experiencing all the frustrations of being foreign in China. Much later I searched several different maps but on not one, except the map we had at the time, did I find any mention of Wanning.

We did have one pleasure to look foward to, and that was seeing Mo Chui Shao again. We had so many questions to ask about Hainan, about the festival, about the tea drying process, and we telephoned him at once as we had promised.

'I am so glad you called me. My father is greatly looking forward to seeing you again. Dinner is all prepared.' He arrived with a friend to escort us there on the backs of their bicycles. Up here on the north coast spring had only just arrived, and the paddy fields – so green and fertile in the south – were only now being ploughed, and flooded by women who laboriously swung buckets back and forth.

We were greeted as old friends by Mr Mo and the manager of the Qiongshan County Foodstuffs Corporation, and immediately provided with a delicious dinner of *jaozi*, ravioli filled with chopped meat and onions and covered in chilli sauce. These were followed by sweets and biscuits and cups of tea.

'Now it is time for dinner.'

'But we've just had dinner!'

'Oh no, that was tea. Please come this way.'

We followed him across the passage to the kitchen, a tiny room shared by four or five families. It was more like a store room than a kitchen, the walls stacked with boxes and papers, leaving only just enough room for three little footstools, and between them on the ground a rice boiler (like a pressure cooker) and an electric ring for the soup.

Chui Shao had gone to great trouble, but we were defeated by the chicken which came whole, still with its feet and its head with pale boiled eyes and boiled coxcomb. With chopsticks, eating chicken still on the bone is extremely difficult, but by now we had mastered the technique of putting the whole thing in the mouth and spitting out the bits, as we had seen it done. Hoping it was the right thing, we spat the bits into the bowls.

'What are you doing?' cried Chui Shao. 'You must spit the bits on to the floor. The bowl is for rice and the floor will be swept.'

It was all rather different from the Xinglong Hot Springs, or the Wanning County Officers' dining room, but even allowing for this and the large tea, Patrick was eating unusually little.

'Didn't you see it?' he asked me afterwards.

'See what?'

'I hoped you hadn't. It was a huge rat, really big. I saw it running out of the papers and along behind you, and then back into the boxes again. I had to sit there in that tiny space knowing it was there.'

A rat! Nothing could be worse. By some stroke of good fortune I never once saw a rat in Asia. A rat ate my soap and my camera cleaning fluid on a beach in Thailand, and I saw plenty squashed into the road in Kathmandu, but never once did I see an actual living rat. It is one of the few advantages of being short-sighted.

We told Chui Shao about the festival, but he did not seem interested. In fact there was little that did interest him except his English studies. He wanted us to make a tape recording, reading a text from his English course so that he could listen and improve his pronunciation; it was all about the terrors of air travel, the fear of customs officers, and also the awfulness of Hong Kong where there are beggars *everywhere*, and everyone is *obsessed* by TV. We tried to explain that the writer had exaggerated a little, but Chui Shao did not want to hear. He was not interested in the content of the text, only in the grammar and vocabulary, and it was towards this goal of improving his English that his entire life was directed. He had not learnt to dance because he wanted to study English; he did not go to the cinema because he wanted to study English. He had left his youth organisation because he needed more time for English. Now he wanted to learn French. I admired his perseverance and determination, but also felt slightly used. We did not mind singing (or speaking) for our supper, but he did not care who or what we were, just as long as he could practise his English. We thought more fondly than ever of Gui Gian, and wished he was here with us. We saw Chui Shao several more times but when we left the island there was no chance to say goodbye as he was deep in conversation with another foreign couple. 'Hainan island is the second largest island in China . . .'

We had to decide on our next destination. Time and money were running out for Patrick, and it was becoming urgent for him to leave China soon. The 'ten days' had of course long passed, but now it was time to leave for the mainland, and go via Guangzhou to Shanghai, and then north to Beijing where Patrick would take the trans-Siberian home. I had something else in mind too, something buried so deep it was little more than a glimmer of a plan, but potentially so huge that I hardly dared acknowledge it even to myself: it was to go to Tibet.

In Hong Kong we had seen an exhibition of photographs taken by a Chinese friend called Tommy Leung. It was only then I learnt that Tibet had, at last, been opened to individual (rather than group) travellers. I suspected then, in front of the pictures of monks and temples and the great Potala palace, mere fragments of the whole, that I would go there myself. How, I did not know, but I eschewed flying. Flying to Lhasa seemed too easy and too quick. I would go with Patrick up to Beijing, then head on west and try to find a bus or truck to take me to Tibet. But I would think about these details later: for the moment China preoccupied me. It was time to leave the island for China proper, the mainland, the cities, the Yangtze, the Grand Canal – all these still awaited us.

Unknown to us, the ship's departure had been brought forward by a day, and by the time we discovered this, it was leaving within the hour. We ran to pack our bags and jumped into a motor-bike side-car taxi for the port, only to find – after much confusion – that it was the wrong port. Our driver had left and not another was in sight; we waited and eventually saw one chugging towards us. We agreed to any price and set off along the sea front. It was much further than we thought. Time was slipping by and we still had not bought our tickets, then the motor bike began to make strange noises. The driver pedalled frantically but it did no good: we were running out of petrol. The port was not even in sight. But a minibus was coming so we leapt out and flagged it down, pushed ourselves and our bags inside, and urged its driver to race for the port. Two minutes to go. The ship was still there, but we had no time to thank our surprised saviour. The ship did not leave for another hour.

It was as overcast when we left as it had been when we arrived. The ship was empty: we were almost the only passengers on board, and we stood alone on deck, escorted out to the grey seas by two wind-surfers who wove patterns around us as Hainan Island, our friends, Sanya, Baoting, Wanning, our paradise days, slid astern and vanished into mist.

– 7 –

Travelling

Past the peasants teetering between the paddy fields in the early frosty light, past the peasants ploughing fields, pushing barrows, chopping wood, and shouldering baskets to return wearily back down the paddies for evening rice: a day evolves into a lifetime for millions as seen from the capsule of a dining-car where we sit beside the chinking soya sauce bottles, looking out.

Guangzhou to Shanghai, thirty-three hours. Our day began with music and lights at 6 a.m., followed by mass ablutions, everyone thrusting their toothbrushes under the same tap at the same time and hanging out to dry their identical orange towels. A faceless, nameless woman addresses us over the Tannoy: now fold your blankets neatly, those descending at the next station have your tickets ready. Along comes the blue-uniformed attendant swinging her black mop over tea leaves and melon-seed husks; up go our feet as she thrusts it under the seats. Fifteen minutes later she is there again: I am surprised how much rubbish she can collect. Here comes the man with the great grey kettle, and out go the mugs for yet another cup of tea. We are travelling in 'hard sleeper' which, like Indian trains, is an open carriage partitioned to provide six-berth compartments. But unlike Indian trains 'hard' does not mean a wooden board, but padded bunks with sheets, blankets, air conditioning, and the attendant with the black mop.

Our return to Guangzhou was not a success. First, it was still raining. Secondly, our hotel, having been empty before, was now full. We were given camp beds in the corridor where we were kept awake and woken early by Chinese men in rubber boots who tramped back and forth, clearing their throats and spitting. Despite not being named in any guide book, the Government Workers' Hostel had become known simply along the travellers' grapevine as *the* cheap place to stay. It always amazed me how quickly word spread. Perhaps someone had put up a note in the infamous Chungking Mansions in Hong Kong, a massive block of sordid cramped hotels housing junkies, forgers, smugglers, dealers, Indian families living in one room, and anyone wanting the latest travel information on China – what restrictions had been lifted, what places were now open to foreigners and so on.

Thirdly, we had to face the dreaded fight for train tickets to Shanghai. It was night and people filled the station, sleeping on baggage in queues that stretched far out into the rain. Dishevelled exhausted people lay on what once had been a garden but was now just a patch of mud from which rose the distinctive smell of sewage. Two art students leant against a tree and sketched the slumbering, waiting, patient Chinese masses.

The first difficulty was finding the right queue, then getting to the front of it and then trying to shout through the narrow window to explain in broken Chinese and by pointing at the phrasebook where we wanted to go. Then – and this was not all – there was the problem of the price, trying to pay student price in people's money and then adding up all the supplements – which type of train, which class, which bunk.

Eventually, triumphant, we left the station with tickets for the 2 p.m. train the next day. We slept late and bade farewell to a Japanese boy sharing our landing, who said he hoped to see us again some day. He did see us again, and sooner than he expected. We arrived at the station to find our train had left six hours earlier: the 2 p.m. train was a different train. We had overlooked the final difficulty, reading the Chinese train ticket.

We were distraught with the foolishness and misery of it,

especially since we had just discovered that neither of us had any money left and were hoping to cash a cheque in Shanghai. We had spent almost our last yuan on buying these tickets. We were determined to get our money back, and forcing our way through the crowds towards the ticket seller, who should we collide with but Len. She was still in her green coat, and still hanging around at the station waiting for travellers to con, but despite our acrimonious parting two months before, we felt as if we had met an old friend. She was embarrassed to see us, and said she was waiting to meet someone coming from Shanghai, though otherwise her story was the same. Her father was still a geography professor, and her boyfriend still a writer for the government (though he was now her fiancé). But though she pretended not to remember where we had met, she agreed to help us.

So began hours of trekking through the pouring rain from one railway building to another, up into the cavernous back regions to meet first the small station manager who waved us to seats while Len tried nervously to explain. It was no good. He sent us on to the big station manager, but he was at lunch. Then down to the special ticket seller, to shout through a door, but one after another they all said no. Finally we had to accept we had lost this money, and more, because of course Len had her price: she needed FEC to buy a Japanese typewriter.

We returned to our hotel shamefaced. The only good thing to emerge from this fiasco – and there had to be something – was an American girl on the station bus who was leaving China and gave me her Taiwan student card. This was forged in Chungking Mansions in a particularly seedy little hotel and was an essential item in mainland China, allowing the traveller to pay local price on trains, in hotels, museums, even restaurants. Thus I became Nina Baumbach of New York. We did not look alike but it never mattered, and later in Beijing two kind friends from Hong Kong sent me my own card with my own photograph on it. With that we could just afford new tickets for tomorrow's train.

This day of misery made the journey itself seem that much more comfortable. Now China was at a pleasant distance outside the dining-car and, with hours of enforced leisure ahead of us, we could at last relax.

– 8 –

Shanghai

It was midnight when we reached Shanghai, a crystal frosted night on the deserted Bund, the only sounds the hooting of the ships as they felt their way up the Huangpu River past warehouses and jagged bones of cranes, and out into the yawning mouth of the Yangtze. Leafless branches glinted white against the silent banking houses and clubs, massive and tomblike, that are the ghostly reminders of the heyday of this city.

By six o'clock in the morning these same streets stream with the unending blue tide of humanity that spills off the pavements and into the bus lanes. Blue caps, blue jackets, blue coats, blue trousers, all identical. Coming up from the more modish south, the blue uniform seems already an anachronism. The flow is broken for a moment by a man who stops, comes to the edge of the bridge to be framed by its iron girders, and searches the distance with his white gloved hand shading his eyes, a white surgical mask across his mouth. Towering behind is the Thirties fortress of Shanghai Mansions, its thick brick walls pocked by black windows. The man drops his arm and is swallowed back into the stream: The Invisible Man; Metropolis.

The stream divides at a park, some people surging on, others descending a few steps to a green retreat beside the river. There the stream breaks up, and the masses become individuals.

An elderly couple in matching white gloves dance slowly together side by side, but never glance at each other. Although they have no music their movements are perfectly synchronised. Around them, in silence, other men and women bend and curve and twist, their gestures fluid yet controlled. They seem almost unaware of each other for their vision is fixed not on the world around them, not even on an inner private world, but on nothingness, on lightness of being, on fusing with the harmony of the universe.

These movements developed over several thousand years out of Daoism to free the *qi*, the life force, in order to establish man's place as a small part of the universe. The *Dao* is the inexpressible source of being, the Way, and this is the principle underlying and controlling the world, of which the *qi*, the vital force of every man, animal, plant or rock, is a part.

By repeating movements and developing a rhythm, the individual comes closer to the rhythm of the world, to the cyclical nature of things. Likewise, physical balance works with the balance of nature. Cross-legged on a bench, his shoes placed neatly beneath him and his head bowed, a man meditates: he is freeing himself and 'sitting in forgetfulness'. Another fights the air with his sword, his dexterity simulating that of an animal. Near the river a man stands alone. Suddenly his body flaps forward and back, out of control as if in a fit until he collapses, exhausted but still twitching. In his mind he can assume the form of an animal – a panther, a monkey, a deer, a crane or a snake – and experience this creature's living, feeding, dying.

Combined with Daoist magic, *Tai qi* was once used to seek immortality both of the *qi* and of the body. In modern China the goal is more mundane, simply to prolong life and live a healthy old age. In the park are classes of old people, several over eighty, bending and stretching with the agility of their children. There are people in the flower beds, amongst the bushes, filling the paths. Now it is eight o'clock and they trickle away to rejoin the stream flowing on to the factories and shops in time for work.

Most hotels had been locked for the night when we arrived

in Shanghai: it was midnight and we had nowhere to go. But a sofa in the lobby of a hotel was offered to us by two young men who, with their tweed jackets, well-bred manners and upper class English accents could have been British public school-boys. I wondered where they had learnt to speak like that; it is almost forty years since the Europeans left. But as I lay in the darkened hallway beside the aquarium, a friendly light shining from their office, I heard two other voices (similar to theirs but more crackly) saying, 'Good morning, I wonder if you would be good enough to look at my car.'

'Certainly Sir.'

'I am afraid my wife crashed it.'

'Oh dear, it looks as though you might need a new body.'

'Perhaps I'd better buy a new car.'

Pause.

'Good afternoon, I see you are selling your house.'

'Yes, do come inside.'

'May I ask how long you have lived here?'

'About twenty years, since 1947.'

'I'm actually looking for a house in the country.'

What more inappropriate bourgeois subjects than repairing a car and buying a house?

It was April Fools' Day, and we were joined on the sofa by a fellow tramp, an Algerian in a black coat, speaking French and trying to explain to a bewildered group that he had left his bottle of wine somewhere. He had arrived on a ship from Marseilles and was drunk, but with the utmost courtesy he was escorted away, one of the police speaking French as perfectly as our receptionists spoke English. Though Shanghai is the industrial hub of China with a huge port and naval base and one of the world's biggest urban populations – twelve million people – it has preserved a delightfully fusty cosmopolitan charm. I loved this city.

We managed to get some more money and celebrated with breakfast (coffee in a silver-plated pot, eggs and bacon on a crested plate) in the massive Peace Hotel, a monument to art deco, a period piece with all its original fixtures and fittings: chandeliers, panelling, lifts, lights. It was once the Cathay Hotel, *the* place to stay when Shanghai was known as the Paris of the East, built by Victor Sassoon who, like many of the foreign merchants, made his fortune out of opium. Everyone who was anyone stayed here – Noël Coward even wrote *Private Lives* here. Later, we drank cocktails and listened to the old jazz band playing *Tea for Two* in the marble bar; there were parties at the Peace Hotel, drinks at the Jinjiang, each more mammoth and splendid than the last. Along the Bund (Wai Tan), Shanghai's one-time Wall Street, are the old Hong Kong and Shanghai Bank, Jardine Matheson and Co., the British Consulate, all long since taken over by the PLA headquarters, the CCP, and the Friendship Store. We heard Chinese rock music playing in the Dongfang Hotel, and wandered inside.

'Sorry, Chinese only.'

This building was once the famous Shanghai Club, so exclusive that it is said an Englishman escaping from a Chinese mob in the 1940s was not allowed to shelter inside until he had been proposed for temporary membership.

Like Guangzhou, Shanghai was opened up as a treaty port in the heart of the tea and silk region after the Opium Wars. The British arrived first, soon to be followed by the French, the Americans and the Japanese who divided the city into concessions, autonomous zones inhabited mostly by Chinese but officially free from Chinese authority. Since the Revolution these concessions have hardly been altered, and are still as distinctive as if in an exhibition of international vernacular styles. The Dutch streets are terraces of redbrick gabled houses; the French, 1920s villas with tall, pitched, shingle roofs and windows set asymmetrically, Thirties pebble-dashed villas, others early modernist, all austerity and clean horizontals and verticals. There is even a lingerie shop – a most shocking sight in China – selling fancy green and mauve padded bras, still with their in-built Forties cups: it is an island of old Europe marooned in China.

Here in the French concession with a friend teaching English to Chinese students we really did have tea for two in some of the dozens of bakeries offering 'cakes à la française' and bowls of sweetened whipped cream – so indulgent, so decadent. They reminded me of cafés in Poland with the same dusty faded colours, the same heavy waitresses, the same look of suspicion from huddles of other students as we mounted the stairs to intrude, too large for the cramped smoky space. These were the cafés once frequented by the White Russian *émigrés* who made up more than half the population of the French concession.

The cafés were also hosts to secret meetings of the underground Communist Party. The CCP was formed in 1921 just around the corner in Xingye Lu, and was constantly under threat from the French police working with the Kuomintang, from Chinese gangs also based here such as the Great Circle Gang, and from the Japanese invaders. Despite being harassed and even massacred the Communists continued their illicit meetings; Zhou En Lai lived here, and his wife Teng Ying Chao worked here with the widow of Sun Yat Sen (who also lived in the French concession) to bring about the liberation of Chinese women.

This must have been a daunting task, for the French concession was not only a refuge for White Russians and political activists, but was also the centre of Shanghai's notorious 'Willow Lane'. By the Revolution there were some 30,000 licensed prostitutes in Shanghai, most of whom worked in the French concession where many brothels fronted as teahouses. These were all closed, and the 'mist and flower maidens' re-educated in the Women's Production and Education Centre, from where they were sent out to work in factories.

Today it is hard to imagine the KMT bully boys, the capitalists, beggars, compradors and opium addicts who once filled these now quiet leafy streets where old women sit in their doorways doing nothing more suspect than enjoying the brilliant winter sun. Above them dangle curtains of washing suspended from poles between balconies and trees. A circle of old men play cards and smoke pipes and turn to call out good-humouredly as we pass. A woman shells prawns and another sits to watch a man bare his foot for the chiropodist. Girls ceaselessly sweep the streets and drive past on a sweeping machine with swivelling brushes. In the central thoroughfares of Nanjing Xilu and Nanjing Donglu, pedestrians, cyclists, Red Flag limousines are all controlled from above by a police-man in a sentry box high up beside the traffic lights. He shouts down at wrongdoers through a megaphone, shaming and sometimes fining them. An old man in a red armband waving a red flag makes sure people spit not on the pavements but into the spittoons that are sunk into the gutters like soup tureens.

Twelve million people: so many that days off are staggered in an attempt to keep the streets relatively clear. It is like this in many Chinese cities, the textile workers free one day, steel workers another. On fine days off, people visit the parks to go out boating between monstrous man-made lotus flowers; to eat ice creams; or to hurtle round and round on roller-skates, the PLA boys hand in hand, policemen helping up girl friends. But what people enjoy most is taking photographs and having photographs taken. Many hire box brownies for the day and so have to use up an entire roll of film which they develop the same afternoon, with pictures of every member of the family positioned in front of every bridge or statue or bush. In many parks photoprops are an added attraction, a car or an aeroplane in which the subject displays himself at the steering wheel, or cardboard models of beautiful ladies and gentlemen in classical dress through which they thrust their own heads.

Another way of passing time, particularly for men, is to sit all day long in teahouses drinking pot after pot of tea while the tables pile high with melon-seed husks, are cleared, and pile up again. The older retired men enjoy themselves and shout and laugh round their tables, but the younger workers sit without speaking much, vacant and weary. However, things are coming to life again, and it was exciting to be here at the start of a cultural renaissance. In the exquisite Huxinting teahouse, at the apex of zigzag bridges in the Chinese quarter, music was provided in the evening by a nine-piece orchestra, the elderly musicians, one a retired policeman, playing together for the first time in twenty years.

Also in fields other than music things were getting going again. We saw an exhibition of new ceramics, described in the accompanying notes as 'not yet good, but a start'. The newest novels were much more wide-ranging and sophisticated than their immediate post-Gang-of-Four predecessors. One 1984 story even mentioned sex. The government was being called on to 'create the necessary conditions, environment and atmosphere' for the exercise of freedom of expression. 'Literary creation is thriving', declared an article in the English-language *Beijing Review*, and 'creation must be free from interference . . . too many derogatory labels were pinned on writers . . . some Party administrators in charge of literature and art were ignorant of artistic professions'. A writer called Wu Zuguang who suffered during the Cultural Revolution declared that the Party's pledge to ensure creative freedom shows 'its maturity, power and self-confidence'.

But practical changes take a long time, and Shanghai still has a notorious housing shortage. On leaving the city we asked a woman the way to the bus station. She had wild matted hair and wore dirty green trousers but she seemed intelligent and took us there. We asked her what time the bus left, pointing at our watches, and she cried, 'Ah!', her eyes brightening, and led us (bowed under the weight of our packs) back the way we had come, along more streets, to . . . a watch shop. Eventually she understood, and helped us to buy tickets for Suzhou. We had several hours to wait, so she kindly invited us home to meet her mother. 'Home' was a *hutong* (an alleyway) of mud-walled hovels, more like stables than houses. The mother was out, so while her daughter went to find her, the woman living opposite invited us in to wait. We sat on stools on the dry earth floor while she cooked lunch outside on a small charcoal burner and some children peered in. The house was just one room divided in half by a wooden platform which was the bed. There was no sanitation, so all washing had to be done at the pump at the end of the street.

The mother bustled up to greet us, a splendid-looking old woman dressed in grey trousers and little black cotton shoes, and she took us across the alley to her identical house. She welcomed us in and gave us tea and sweets, picking out the best ones for us from a plastic bag. Then the two of them, mother and daughter, escorted us back to the station (the mother linking her arm through mine), found our seats, gave us the name of a brother-in-law who worked at Wuxi station, and bade us goodbye. These women, one so seedy-looking, the other living in this squalid overcrowded place, have a brother and a son with a fellowship in the English Department of the University of Ottawa. They showed us his letters, postmarked Ottawa, to prove it.

Gui Gian, sheepish in his sailor's uniform, Wanning.

Gui Gian's mother.

'I love you' were the only words we had in common.

Old and young alike were entranced by the paper dragons.

Over sixty thousand villagers flooded Wanning for the Lantern Festival . . .

. . . to be astonished by two extraordinary foreigners in their midst.

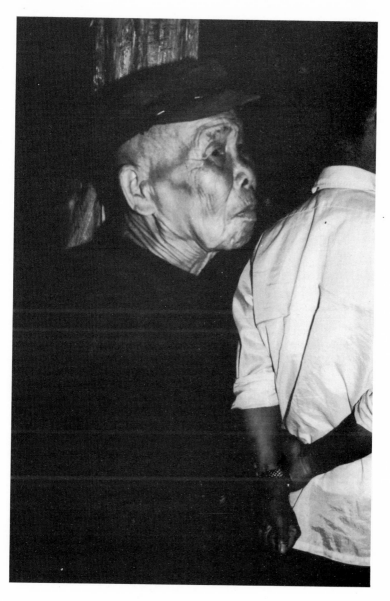

Old man watching the floats.

Armatures suspended this small girl during the days and nights of processions.

Shanghai Mansions, thirties fortress.

Relaxing after a hard day's work, Shanghai.

– 9 –

Suzhou and Beijing

Suzhou is a town of amphibians who live on and off the canals that bisect and enclose it. Small brick houses drop straight into water and a woman leans from a window to scrub out her night soil bucket with bundles of sticks; another lights a stove in an old blackened boat moored alongside which rocks up and down in the wash of others. Lining the canals and the narrow roads are pollarded willows and weeping willows and stocky French plane trees with arching branches that shelter the pavements from a little of the rain.

It is a lively, pretty place on the Grand Canal, (the oldest and longest man-made waterway in the world,) and a great favourite with Chinese tourists. In the main bazaar shops sell bright pink cakes, ink grinders and calligraphy brushes, dumplings – *dim sum* – white and green, boiled, fried and steamed. There is a Daoist temple that has now become a crafts supermarket rather to the dismay, I imagine, of an ancient monk with a wizened face and sunken haunted eyes who sits alone in a cell near the altar. A teashop is taken over by a wedding party and next door clothes are modelled by dummies with amputated legs. It was all this that distracted us on our way to the Twin Pagoda Temple that rises vertically out of the geometrical crisscross lines and squares of streets and water.

Between them are the pleasure gardens built over several hundred years by Chinese aristocrats and officials, reaching their peak during the fifteenth and eighteenth centuries. The summit of modern Chinese art and culture seems to coincide with that of Europe. These are the most celebrated gardens in China, the Plain Man's Politics Garden, the Lion's Grove, the Surging Wave Pavilion, the Garden for Lingering In, the Master of the Nets, the Garden of Harmony, all with their rockeries and creamy magnolias and lakes, moon gates, pavilions, dragons and goldfish. Houses range around, with empty rooms and high polished pillars and latticed wood windows. It was through gardens such as these that Chia Cheng in the Qing dynasty novel *A Dream of Red Mansions* processed with his son Pao-yu and their troupe of sycophantic secretaries dreaming up romantic and suitable names for the different view points.

It always comes as a delightful surprise when a world familiar from a book, or from a hundred paintings, comes to life. Here in these gardens I was walking through a landscape I had seen in every museum on scrolls, on lacquerwork, on embroidery, on porcelain. As I paused to look through the frame of a circular moon gate across ponds and lotus leaves, or rested in a pavilion at the end of a promontory, so I glimpsed the different shifting perspectives of the paintings in which a mountain or river is seen from different levels and angles, foreshortened, heightened, flattened, lengthened. The eye almost walks through a Chinese painting. Here were the same motifs of water, rocks, bamboo, curling eaves, and poetic inscriptions. Only missing were the artist's own chop print hanging in the sky; and the people dwarfed by towering cliffs, the robed and embroidered scholars with their topknots and trailing beards, and the ladies with white-powdered cheeks and moth eyebrows and small waists and necks as slender as the clasp of a courtier's buckle.

Also missing were the precipitous mountains, but the essence, the *qi* of those mountains was there, expressed in the bulging limestone rockeries. These gardens are not the inspiration for Chinese landscape painting but are inspired by it, and if not by particular works, then by the same ideals of a harmony of earth and water, of yin and yang. Chinese art is not one of mimesis; landscape painting does not portray a particular place, or a time of day, or a single point of view, but aims to express the essence of a place. As the pavilions are for pausing and looking and contemplating, so the empty spaces in a painting of the 'Southern' Daoist or Chan Buddhist school suggest the void, sitting in forgetfulness, action through non-action, harmony of the *qi* with nature.

Yet paradoxically these gardens are completely unnatural with their walkways and jaunty bridges and imported rocks and clever arrangements of mirrors. The Chinese dislike and fear wildness, they like to capture and tame.

Bonzais with their clipped roots and stunted exquisite branches are what they admire and cultivate; hence too bound feet (brutality and delicacy), and here in these gardens for the first time I saw elderly women tottering on their tiny wedge-shaped feet encased in grey slippers, more like little hooves than feet, and I was shocked by such a visible and poignant reminder of the old regime.

Not far away from these gardens is another very different China, one not portrayable in delicate brush marks but more suitable for the coarse woodcuts of a Revolutionary artist like Yang Nawei. We looked for the moat that surrounds the city and found it after picking our way down a mud track, past a ruined pagoda standing forlornly in a scrap yard beneath grey skies, and slithering up on to the old city fortifications. Below was the sludge-coloured water churning between warehouses and factories. It was busy with boats, mostly long open barges, some motorised, others rowed with one paddle from the stern which looked hard work as they toiled upstream against the current. Some were defeated and were swept back under a bridge, chaotically entangled with other boats heading up-stream.

Up a small side canal, where the water was black and thick as tar, came a boat much like all the others, heaved along by a man and a woman wearing brown rubber boots. They moored

beside a small house and, looking purposeful, the man disappeared. He returned with a hose pipe, one end of which he
stuck into an underground tank, the other end into the open
boat. Out pumped gallons of sewage, night soil, taken off as
fertiliser for the fields. I pitied this couple – and all these
people – their dismal lives untouched by any of the well-
publicised reforms.

In a row between the factories and the canals they were
polluting crouched tiny hovels. Outside them in the drizzle
women sheltered under raincoats to cook on their charcoal
stoves. We clambered up a grass bank above them and watched
men unloading earth from barges into carts which, like beasts
of burden, they dragged uphill towards the pagoda with ropes
cutting into their naked shoulders. A boy by a *jaozi* stall looked
surprised to see us.

'What are you doing here?' he asked.

'Having a look.'

We went to a free market on one of the bridges (Marco Polo
described the 'Six thousand bridges of stone in this city'). I
stood on a wall to take a photograph, and found I was hemmed
in by curious people. Patrick walked away.

'Don't go!' I begged.

He smiled scornfully. 'Good training for being alone.' The
ground lurched away below me, I was rising up as high as a
satellite, looking down on myself as a speck lost and alone
among millions of strangers in a vast land that was huger, older,
more powerful, more complex than I in my ignorance had ever
imagined. Panic, vertigo, a pathetic smallness: these were what
I felt. I did not have to go to Tibet, I could go home whenever I
wanted, but England was a world away and this state of
travelling was now my life. I was afraid, but determined not to
be. With only a week or so before Patrick was due to leave, I had
to get used to being without him forever shielding and support-
ing me, but time for us was running out and we had taken to
spending almost every minute together. I was torn between
clinging on until the last moment and leaving now, for I would

rather have done the leaving than be left; I saw myself standing forlornly on the station waving him off, and I hated this vision more than anything. But I could not steel myself to go first.

Slowly we made our way north to the eerie blank boulevards of Beijing. Pompous thoroughfares escorted by grey modernist buildings marched off in parallel lines to the distance where they dwindled to nothing, to wasteland. The pallid sunlight of early spring on the still skeletal trees only added to the overall chill. Distances were huge: we went to the poste restante hoping for warming letters from home but were ensnared so tightly in the bus that the automatic door slammed shut before we could disentangle ourselves, and so missed our stop. When we did escape, bruised and dishevelled, we had to walk back for over a mile.

The columns of cyclists were two blue strips, so dense and unbroken as to appear stationary, that flanked the otherwise empty avenues. But for a muffled whirr of thin tyres on tarmac and the ringing of a thousand small bells, the streets were silent. Even the people were muffled, the lower halves of their faces covered with white surgical masks, and their heads swathed in white cotton hats. Some were hidden behind dark glasses, like Mafiosi surgeons, if there could be such a thing.

In the bleak expanse of Tiananmen Square – the heart of Beijing and the heart of all China – Mao's portrait still reigns supreme. It hangs on the Gate of Heavenly Peace from where he proclaimed the People's Republic of China in October 1949. How long he will remain there, overlooking his own mausoleum, is anyone's guess. In the Great Hall of the People that forms one side of the square a meeting of the CCP was taking place to condemn the spiritual and economic pollution arising out of the new liberal regime: perhaps Mao is not completely dead.

Walls of people built up along the pavements behind the linked arms of the police: the delegates swept past in a cavalcade of curtained limousines but there was not a wave, not a chink of a face. Security hid them from the masses as firmly as the Emperor in his sedan chair on the rare occasions he emerged from his Forbidden City into that same square. The cars passed, and passively the people flowed on. They were not disappointed: they had not gathered to see the leaders but were just those the police had stopped, momentarily, from crossing the road.

Behind loomed the great red walls of the secret city, its miles measured out by the spying eyes of watch-towers. Unauthorised entry to this imperial palace-fortress was once punishable by death; now it is open to all, to the ten thousand people who flock here each day. Looking down from Jing Shan on hall after hall, gate after gate, the orange brown roofs with their curling corners were as weightless as crisp autumn leaves. At the ends of many of these eaves are little mounted figures and animals, the figure a tyrant who was supposedly hung here, and the animals who blocked his escape.

The other great sights – the Temple of Heaven, the Ming Tombs, the Summer Palace – have receded into a haze of preparations for our separate departures. We visited embassies, bought visas, telexed for money, and I went to the Public Security Bureau to collect my Alien's Travel Permit stamped for Datong and Lhasa. They were both semi-closed places; Datong was to be the first stop on my journey west, and Lhasa, though I did not know it then, was to be my last. I had not yet finally decided to go to Tibet; I felt too superstitious to admit to myself how much I wanted to go, in case it did not happen. 'Going to Tibet' was still a mere flicker; I feared that if I tried to fan it into a blaze, I might blow it out. But I had discovered something that could be an exciting possibility. Only one month before I arrived in China the government had officially opened the border between Tibet and Nepal to foreigners. Border controls had earlier relaxed for Nepalese traders and Tibetans living in exile, but this was the first time since the Chinese occupied Tibet in 1959 that foreigners could use this 'exit point'. Even before Chinese rule, this border was sealed off, some say by the Tibetans and others by the British, and any unauthorised foreigners entering Tibet were immediately expelled, even shot. But now it was possible not only to go to Lhasa, but also to leave the country for Nepal and thence for India. That meant I could go overland all the way from Hong Kong back to Kathmandu, where I had been eight months earlier, thus completing a huge loop through Asia. But I would have to reach Tibet first, and then see if it could be done. Hedging my bets, I booked myself a seat on the trans-Siberian for two months' time.

Before I had even left Beijing, however, I had come to hate that train. Eight of us shared a dormitory in the TV room of a hotel – the camp beds put up at 11.45 p.m. after the TV was switched off, and put away by 5.30 a.m. in time for conferences – and everyone but me was leaving now, on the trans-Siberian. I felt as if I was the only foreigner staying on. The train was taking Patrick back to the far-away world of his family and friends and girl friend. And I feared that once reabsorbed into his own society he would forget our days together. We made no plans to meet again. He was leaving at dawn the next morning and the evening before, our final evening, we argued passionately and shouted in the streets. Then we rode back to the hotel standing cheek to cheek in the bus, weary and sad.

– Part II –

– 10 –

Datong

When the moment came it was subdued, even lighthearted, and as I waved him off I felt a thrill of anticipation that my own journey was just beginning.

I looked around the station waiting-room as though seeing it for the first time. Everything had shifted into sharper focus. A unit of railway guards gathered for a lecture from their leader, the girls at the back shuffling their feet and giggling, and then asked me to move so they could hang a banner over the seats: a delegation of TV manufacturers was arriving. I had half an hour until my train to Datong. I wondered if they all knew I was alone; but how could they? My voice in my head grew loud.

A soldier sprang up to help lift my pack on to the luggage rack. No one spoke English so I was left to myself for a while, until we ran alongside the Great Wall as it twisted and spun this way and that. Then even the most dignified passengers dodged from window to window as they spotted another segment like the vertebrae of one of the thousands of imperial dragons that adorn every stone staircase and spirit screen and roof-top in the Forbidden City. This dragon's back lay across the whole of northern China, linking the east coast with Jaiyuguan in Gansu province nearly two thousand miles away, and supposedly keeping out the marauding hordes of Mongols descending from the north. Datong lies just south of the wall and during the Qin, Han and Northern Wei dynasties had been a frontier town, protecting the then political and cultural heart of China.

For two years the Great Wall kept Genghis Khan at bay; we

passed briefly behind it into Inner Mongolia from where he came, and then turned south into Shanxi province. Bare brown mountains and valleys were cracked apart by canyons, great jagged furrows across the earth, like a giant version of the Chinese biscuits I had bought. I wished that Patrick could have seen it, and then remembered that of course he had passed this way only half an hour earlier on the first stage of his journey before heading north to Ulan Bator. I thought about him and how exposed I felt without him, and thought: here I am, completely alone in the middle of China and no one but he knows where I am or where I am going. What is awaiting me? What adventures? What boredom? What loneliness? What happiness?

We entered the heart of China's coal mining area – black cities, smog, open-cast mines, slag heaps – and after eight hours reached Datong. Feeling peculiarly disorientated I took a bus to the hotel, an imposing building set amongst grass and trees up a long drive. Could this really be it? It looked more like an official government building, with guards at the gates. Small and insignificant under my pack I walked past them and up the drive and met a uniformed attendant who showed me to a girls' dormitory. It was deserted but in an annexe I noticed some bags and a copy of *Son of the Revolution* and felt cheered by the possibility of a sympathetic person staying here.

I was hungry and went downstairs to find the restaurant. I sat at a large table in an empty room, only to be told I could not stay there as it was for Chinese only. The Western dining room was a daunting sight. There were more round tables, large enough for eight, and several were already occupied. They were too big to sit at alone. I steeled myself to go in. Most of the guests were from tour groups, but I noticed a table of scruffier people, people like me, and a girl who smiled in a friendly way. I forced myself to speak and asked if I could use a student card here and through a haze of self-consciousness heard her say Yes. But that exhausted my supply of courage and I left the room. Everyone was staring. I walked away down the corridor, trembling, and leant against the wall: the strain of the parting, of the long day, of lack of food were suddenly too much. I considered returning to the lonely dormitory and hiding there, but I was being absurd, there was nothing to fear, and I went back in. I took hold of a chair.

'Yes,' said a curly-haired man who seemed to be in charge, 'do join us.'

Close to tears, my voice shaking, I sat down, and the girl who had smiled before smiled again. The man was English and vaguely reminded me of someone though I could not think who. For some reason the others at the table went quiet and as we talked across it – where we had been, where we were going, the usual things – they listened. He said he was studying Chinese at Beijing Daxue, and the smiling girl was his sister who had come to visit him. She called him Daniel, and he came from the Polytechnic of Central London. Did I suspect then? He asked me about myself. Half to me and half to his sister he said, 'Someone called Helena lived in our house.'

'Yes,' I said, 'that was me.'

We all laughed in astonishment as he and I simultaneously recognised each other.

'You're Danny Alberman aren't you?' I could hardly believe it. I had spent one month living in his parents' house in Highgate, and as rent, sitting with their 90-year-old aunt for a few hours a day. Danny had shown me round the house and garden before disappearing to Paris, and his sister, Catty, was away in Israel at the time. I had heard how lovely she was, and it was true; it was she who was reading *Son of the Revolution*. After dinner we drank tea together and laughed until we cried about some of the funnier Chinese habits. Catty moved her things into the dormitory and we talked late into the night.

With an American called Steve who also had been at our table we visited Xuanlong Hanging Monastery. It was a long way outside Datong and officially closed to foreigners except on tours, but Danny, a fluent Chinese speaker, seemed to open all doors and with no trouble we managed to get bus tickets. We had a two-hour wait, so wandered in the main street trying on the Fifties tortoiseshell sunglasses on sale everywhere, watching impromptu street magic, and a troupe of blind musicians performing excerpts from local opera, the crowd delighted by a man impersonating an old widow. One of them, a young woman with two long straight plaits stood alone with her hands behind her back and her eyes fixed on the distance. She sang with a fierce rasping passion that echoed the harsh scraping of the primitive two-stringed instruments.

The cold wind was piercing so we escaped inside a building called 'Fairyland'. A drawing of a bowl and chopsticks indicated a restaurant downstairs and we descended down and down, eight or nine flights, until at last we reached three long tunnels with arched ceilings and tables at which people were eating. A subterranean steamy restaurant, it must have been a bomb shelter, part of an underground city like the one that stretches beneath Beijing, built to withstand a possible Soviet attack in the 1960s.

The journey to the monastery was through some of the most dramatic country I had yet seen, similar to the train ride but now high up in the barren Heng mountains. Loess-walled villages were grafted on to the flat tops of plunging canyons, the same yellow-ochre as the earth from which they were made. Loess is the crystalline wind-blown soil that flies in from the Gobi Desert and covers everything in a fine layer of dust. Some houses were even carved out of the earth, cave dwellings with curved tunnel entrances like 'Fairyland'. We paused in one village for *jaozi*, and the men were fascinated by my single ear-ring, assuming I must be a member of a special sect. They were disappointed to learn it was simply all I had, and actually a fishing swivel someone had given me.

The monastery was a series of tiny temples, not hanging but perched on stilts half-way up a precipice, clinging to the rock face like a bird's nest. It was a remarkable piece of engineering, originally built 1,400 years ago; somehow it had survived earthquakes and the Red Guards. Though the sun shone, the cold was intense, and the wind whipped up the gorge shaking the frail suspension bridge as we crossed. There were no monks here now but we found an attendant dozing with his friends on their *kang*, a wide brick bed covered with a straw mat, that filled half the room and was heated from beneath by a wood fire. He unlocked some doors and hurried back to the warmth, while we climbed along the narrow parapets and balustrades suspended over the sheer drop, into temples that were grottoes of brightly painted plaster Buddhas and deities and devils, mostly two or three feet high, all gathered beneath pink and white plaster clouds. As the tourist leaflet said, 'To wander up and down the suspending stairways, the winding corridors and the plankways . . . one might feel like drifting in a dreamlike world.'

There was no bus back to Datong, so while we waited for something to pass by, we lay on a roadworker's warm *kang* in his roadside shelter. He told me that in summer the mountains turned light green, but I found it hard to imagine anything growing here. A bus passed and we flagged it down; it was a commune bus returning to Hunyuan, the village where we had had lunch, and the workers smiled a lot and pressed cigarettes on us.

The girls at the *zhaodaisuo* were most welcoming and immediately fetched thermoses of hot water while I got quickly under the quilts to warm up. Two Chinese men touring the area invited us to have supper with them; I had already seen the apologies for meat hunks of bluish bone) that were on sale alongside the dusty road, so I wondered what we were eating, and where it had come from. As the dishes piled higher, so the crowd around us grew. I thought they were just curious, the usual staring crowd, but before we had even left the table the old men had darted forward to snatch up the leftovers in their hands and hungrily fill their mouths. Here, far from the tourist route, and far from the towns, people were starving. The only similar thing I had seen was in Beijing (the heart of the tourist route) where old men and children stole empty beer jugs off the tables and took them back to the counter to get the deposit before the diner noticed. But it was not only the Chinese who were hungry. Also in Beijing I had seen an English traveller charming some American ladies, telling them about his exploits. They were most impressed. As soon as they left, he grabbed the remains off their plates, stuffing them into his mouth with his hands, dropping them in his urgency, much to the amazement of the Chinese waitresses who giggled together behind a screen.

There were signs of one-time prosperity in Hunyuan. Remains of grand houses with carved doors led to courtyards and one-storey houses, extended to accommodate the family as it grew, but were now the homes of several different families. Though all the walls were built of compact loess or adobe, bricks of earth and straw, the roofs were tiled with upturned eaves sometimes decorated with sinuous dragons. Our evening stroll through these *hutongs* inevitably became a pied piper procession, and there was particular excitement when we entered a shop. The local English teacher was brought to meet us but was so overwhelmed, completely shredding the piece of paper she had twisted round her fingers, that she could hardly utter a word. Maoist slogans daubed on the walls had been whitewashed over; Danny, a fund of information, said that during the Cultural Revolution when to criticise Mao was blasphemy, people would simply point at their chins to suggest Mao's dimple.

It was another long bus journey, this time over rough unsurfaced roads across a dusty plain, to Yingxian Wooden Pagoda, the self-proclaimed oldest multi-storey wooden structure in China, built in about AD 1056. It was still early when we arrived so we had the nine storeys with their ancient murals and Buddhist statues to ourselves. As the tourist leaflet here said: 'Here the tourists stand in fine view of distant objects.' I looked down on the miles of tin-roofed workers' houses, and a school yard filling up with children who ordered themselves into a pattern to bend and stretch in time with a woman's voice that crackled out of the radio each morning. We recorded our visit with a group photograph taken by a professional with a box brownie in front of a painted backdrop of a Chinese garden.

That evening I waved off Dan and Catty who were returning to Beijing. Now, after a temporary (and welcome) hitch, my break was complete. I would miss them, and even more I would miss Patrick, but I also rejoiced in being alone again, in taking my own life into my own hands, shaping my days myself. I was free.

The main object of my visit to Datong was the fifth century Yungang Buddhist caves, built when Datong was a capital of the Northern Wei dynasty ruled by a Turkish-speaking people called the Toba. Buddhist teachings began to take so firm a hold at this time that Buddhism was proclaimed a state religion. While the great days of Chinese civilisation were just beginning – the Grand Canal, the rise of the mandarins and of poetry and painting – so another civilisation was coming to an end: Rome was sacked by the Barbarians.

I took a series of buses along a railway line: China's steam engines are produced here in Datong, and smoke from the trains combined with the black and yellow effluent that gushed without restraint from a string of factories. Typical of a developing country, the environment is not high on the list of priorities. Beside these heavy industries stood ancient villages and behind them, carved into the hillside, the caves. I was dismayed. I had expected these works of Buddhist art to be buried in some remote mountainside, and wondered how long they could withstand the corrosive pollution.

But this threat made them seem paradoxically strong, the ancient Buddhas vulnerable yet dignified as they gazed over this modern wasteland. Fifty-three caves, said to contain over 50,000 statues: some were high and dank, majestic as cathedrals, and carved in relief with stories of Buddha's life. There were Bodhisattvas, Buddhas who have attained enlightenment but rejected it to help guide others to the same nirvana;

and the Maitreya or future Buddha, all interspersed with bodhi trees and deities and flying 'angels'. Much of it was surprisingly Byzantine, with rows of kneeling figures whose hands were clasped in prayer and heads ringed with haloes. Others resembled Hindu sculpture (cave art originally came from India) with many-armed and headed Vishnus, and Shiva with his trident; but there were also Chinese dragons and pagodas. It was a collision of different styles. Several caves were filled with a single solid almost three-dimensional Buddha, standing, sitting on a lotus, some so huge that only their feet were visible in one cave while high up above in another cave appeared their heads and shoulders.

By now I had seen thousands of Buddha images, and I was to see many more, but each was different, some smiling to themselves, some stern, some serene, some smug. The most smug were in Ladakh and the most boyish in Burma. Some are thick-lipped and jewelled, some are patched all over with gold leaf, some have blue corkscrew hair, and all have the long-lobed ears that were dragged down by the heavy jewellery that Siddhārtha Gautama wore as prince of the Sakya before he rejected this princely life to become a Buddha. It is ironic that Buddha's dying wish was that he should not be worshipped and that images in his likeness should not be made. His wish was granted for five hundred years, until sculptors and painters could no longer restrain themselves.

Alone now, I felt so alive, as though I had at last emerged from a too-warm room out into sharp cold air, and all my sleeping senses had woken. Every feeling became more intense, more intensely joyous but also, if anything went wrong, more intensely awful. Though I was now free to spend the day as I chose, in other ways I was less free than before. I became more susceptible, for example, to the constant staring, and less tolerant. Outside the Red Flag department store I saw a Muslim in a skull cap who must have come east from Xinjiang to sell sultanas; he was constantly smothered by fascinated Hans who had probably never seen his like, though they were citizens of the same country, and he grew angry and shouted at them to leave him alone. We caught each other's eye: I knew just how he felt. I also minded more when people were unfriendly. It was hard to know how to react to the surly shop assistants who sat behind their counters filing their nails and looking furious when I distracted them, angrily clacking at their abacus. Patrick used to lean over, put his two index fingers at the corners of his mouth, and lift it into a grotesque smile. They could never resist it, but somehow this trick did not work so well without him.

But it was a thrill of self-motivation, almost of power, to be able to say, Today I am going to Xian, and simply because I want to, not because someone suggested it, not to meet someone there, but simply because I have decided to go there. To be entirely and single-mindedly responsible for my own actions: this was exciting. I had a book of Suzuki's teachings, and perhaps I was influenced by reading (or misreading) about Buddhism and the escape from dualism. Each action must be undertaken with the 'single mind' and must be a complete self-contained thing that need have no cause or purpose beyond itself. I was going to Xian because I was going to Xian. Each action is important in itself, I read. With this theory, no action need be a wasted action provided I was committed to it. So now I need not regret any decision, spontaneity is all, and motives need not be ulterior. I had visions of life as a series of free-floating actions that bobbed independently but with equal weight in a kind of limbo; and the assumption that every action must in some way be made use of and lead to another action, not be allowed to float free, began to seem almost repulsive.

This strength and control were just a few of the things Bodhidharma had taught would lead to enlightenment. He believed enlightenment could come as a flash and last only a few seconds at any time in one's life, and not after years of 'right actions' as had been thought before. Nirvana can alight as we walk down the street or sit beside a river, at any moment as long as we are intensely living ourselves, for he believed that each one of us contains the 'Buddha nature' and simply have to realise it.

With no one to bring me out of day-dreams such as this my eyes glazed over and I saw nothing around me. I walked and stood in front of temples and people and shops, I took the bus, but I was conscious of seeing none of it. Conversations in my head grew so animated that sometimes I caught myself speaking out loud to some imaginary figure or to Patrick, even laughing. An old woman must have felt sorry for me, or thought I was crazy, for she took me in tow round the twelfth century Huayuan Monastery, but it did not help, and I am left with only the haziest memory of the biggest Buddhist hall in China.

Datong to Xian: I had twenty-four hours of travelling ahead of me, sitting on a hard wooden seat with a straight wooden back, unable to move since there was no way I could get out of the carriage and back again without being crushed. But I enjoyed the journey: I had a window seat and friendly people to talk to. A nineteen-year-old student of economics spoke a few words of English, and with the help of my dictionary and a lot of hard work we could understand each other a little. On a scrap of paper he wrote: 'England black amber dismiss very muck worker hard by now.' I worked out that 'black amber' meant coal, 'dismiss' meant strike, and 'very muck' meant very much. He wanted to talk about the miners' strike. There are no strikes in China, he said. Then he wrote:

'Go speek our think'.

Again I traced his words in my dictionary, and understood that he wanted to know more about Speaker's Corner. He could not believe the police do not intervene.

An older man introduced himself and welcomed me to China. He spoke much better English but asked the string of usual questions: are you married, how much do you earn, may I know your nationality, what is the price of your watch? He had a phrase book, the *Railway Worker's Conversation Book*, that had all these questions in it. We leafed through the book together and came to a section about the Party working for the people and the people working for the Party towards the glory of the realisation of socialism.

'That not good,' he said hastily, and refused to let me read it, flipping over to the next part.

'Where did you learn your English?' I asked him.

'I learnt it by myself, and from watching TV.'

'Do you watch "Follow Me", the BBC language programme?'

'Yes! That very good.'

'With Katherine Flower?'

'Yes! You know her?'

'No, I've seen her on TV too.'

He was disappointed. This language programme must be one of the most popular programmes in China, and the presenter Katherine Flower something of a star. Everyone watches it, before and after work as everyone it seems wants to learn English. It is *the* craze at the moment. Foreigners are always being approached.

'Excuse me, I would like to speak with you because I want to practise my English.' No question of pretending that they like the look of you; they are known by the foreign students as the Language Rapists. I tried not to be impatient as for many it is the first time they have ever had the chance to use the language they have struggled to learn.

But this man genuinely did want to have a conversation. He too was an economist, on his way to a conference in Taiyuan, yet he said he earned only fifty yuan per month (less than twenty pounds), however his house cost only three yuan per month, and a bowl of *jaozi* only 0.08 yen (eight fen). He said he had met several foreigners and had found the British more reserved than the Americans. 'Is it true that English people do not like to be asked if they are married, or how much they earn?'

'Yes, I think it is true.'

'But why?'

I began to explain about privacy, but as I looked up at the crowd gathered around us, I knew he would never understand. Privacy is a concept totally alien to the Chinese mind. In traditional extended families everyone lived together, the wives working for the mother-in-law, the cousins brought up together. There was little place for the individual family unit living in private. In *A Dream of Red Mansions*, Pao-yu, though no longer a child, is forever running in and out of his girl cousins' room, lying down on their *kangs*, helping them dress, and all their relationships are conducted before a host of servants, pages and slaves. Then, in the days of communes, there was no private ownership and individualism was despised. Families lived in barracks, and sometimes even husbands and wives were segregated into single sex dormitories. Now the problems are more to do with shortage of living space, different families sharing cramped accommodation and kitchens and bathrooms, their children brought up together in the unit where their parents work.

Above all there is no sense of personal space, no taboos about standing close together, intruding, coming up to stare. For someone from the West, and particularly from England, this is one of the hardest things to get accustomed to. The public loos, for example, are long ditches over which people squat, face to bottom. The arrival of a foreigner causes great excitement, and the women gather round to watch, pointing things out to each other without the slightest inhibition. Red haired women, I heard, suffer terribly. In more up-market hotels where individual loos are behind doors, people rarely bother to shut them while they chat to each other. In our hotel in Suzhou there was an attempt at privacy, and a wall had been built around the loo which stood in the middle of the bathroom. But this wall was only three feet high, so there people sat in the centre of the room with their heads sticking out over the top, and no one seemed to mind.

We had only just left Datong when there was a flurry of excitement at the carriage door. A young Chinese girl broke through the bodies and clasped my hand in hers to tell me how delighted she was to meet me.

'My name is Miss Margaret. I have come to beg you to do me the honour of accompanying me to meet my class mates. They would be very honoured to meet you.'

'Of course,' I said, and was hauled by the hand through several carriages to meet Mr Wong, Miss Li, Mr Xie, Mr Yang and several others, about twelve in all. They were the English class from Datong Teacher Training College, off on a Sunday outing, and never before had they met a 'native speaker'.

'This is our golden opportunity to speak to an English person,' they chorused. 'The years of one's youth are the golden years to study.'

They asked for my impressions of China.

'Yes, yes, and we think England is a very beautiful country too. Please tell us, what does a young man like us, of twenty-two years old, do in your country?' I assured them that twenty-two-year-old young men in England were just like them: hard-working and eager to embark on the golden years of life. Questions came so fast there was hardly time to answer before another spilled out. They begged me to sing a song, so I sang such universally known songs as *Jingle Bells* and *Home on the Range* which they could join in. They also knew *Che Sera* and the theme from *Love Story – Love Story* and *On Golden Pond* were their favourite films. The other Chinese passengers looked on at their golden Chinese youth and smiled indulgently.

When we reached their stop, Miss Margaret took me once more by the hand, took my bag, and led me back down the train to my seat. The others collected beneath my window to wave goodbye.

All day long my fellow travellers and I spoke; when one tired the other took over, everything I said translated to the crowd.

Yes you speak very good English, yes you speak better English than he does. By the time we reached Taiyuan where I had to change trains I was drained, shattered. I walked out of the station determined to see all I could of Taiyuan in the few hours I had, but a blast of dust-filled wind hit me and got in behind my contact lenses, so I gave up and returned to the station to seek out the delicious seclusion of the first-class waiting room, into which foreigners of whatever class are allowed. I had to ring a bell to be let in, and I lay down across some seats to retreat into the private world of my walkman. This was when Patrick and I, too tired to read or write, would have escaped together to talk and make plans. The walkman was no substitute, but it was better than nothing.

As usual there was an appalling dog-like fight to get on the train, everyone pushing, tearing at each other's clothes, knocking people aside in their frenzy to get to the seats. Unlike many of them, I at least had a reserved seat, and though someone was sitting in it, he moved with alacrity when I arrived, and helped me lift up my bag. (Not that it was heavy: I had long ago discarded all but my most precious possessions.) Despite a certain level of equality between men and women – women drive buses, build roads, wear the same clothes as men – I often noticed a great courtesy towards women, and not just foreign women. This, however, vanished when it came to getting on the train and women, children, old people, cripples, anyone was knocked out of the way.

Sharing my corner was a smiling old couple who had the politeness to lean out of the window to spit, though once the train had left they shut the window to keep out the soot, and proceeded to spit anywhere. Spitting is the national disease. Fortunately it is preceded by a loud gurgle and clearing of the throat which allows you to move your foot and look the other way. Everyone does it; perhaps they all suffer from the loess in the air released by the Gobi Desert and generations of defor-estation. Though there is now a massive tree-planting drive, it will take many centuries before the trees lost in this century alone are replaced. Perhaps the men spit because they smoke too much. Perhaps it is because they are disgusted by the Western habit of nose-blowing and returning the used hand-kerchief to the pocket. Perhaps it is simply a habit. Only that day I had read in the *China Daily* of a new attempt to ban public spitting in Beijing.

Anyone caught spitting in public places in Beijing will face a fine of 50 fen, together with a public dressing down and cleaning of the floor.

The article went on to announce that 'Factories are producing specially designed toilet paper for habitual spitters.' Spitting never seemed intended as an insult. A man would spit in my direction, smear it in with his shoe, and then smile and ask if he could help me find my way. Throughout a lavish and richly-coloured production of Beijing opera, people would talk and laugh and of course hawk, without making the slightest attempt to muffle the noise, enjoying the opera hugely at the same time. Later, in Xian, I went to a concert of Tang dynasty music given by a troupe of highly skilled musicians. The audience was, I thought, entirely foreigners who were entranced by the cos-tumes and the playing. During one particularly beautiful harp solo, everyone was hushed and motionless until, garg-ling out from the back of the auditorium, came that familiar sound.

Several carriage guards worked hard to get people to their seats, find others floor space nearest the tables on which they could rest their heads, and fit others into the draughty places where the carriages join. Then almost before we had left, they forced the walls of people apart with their kettles of boiling water, some people drinking plain boiled water from their lidded mugs or jam jars, the richer ones enjoying the luxury of tea leaves which were re-used time and again. My neighbours and I exchanged samples of my Hainan Sun River tea for their Jiangsu Cloud Fog tea, and we discussed their relative merits.

Another trolley struggled past, this one with comic books to rent and polystyrene boxes of rice and pork fat. I was beginning to wonder if Chinese pigs were made entirely of fat, for I never saw any meat. I had taken to living on *dofu* (bean curd); the only fruit I saw was bruised and unappetising. Some days I did not eat at all.

I looked round at the wind-roughened faces and coarse utility clothing and wondered how all of us would survive the night of acute discomfort we had ahead of us. The air was already fetid and the floor already slippery. Suddenly I knew I could not stay here. I would try to find a free hard sleeper, even though I had been refused one at the ticket office. I left my pack and pushed and squeezed and shoved my way down the carriage, people having to get up off the floor and lean back on each other as I heaved myself through one carriage, then another and another. Six carriages I passed before reaching 'hard sleeper' and as I passed, so every face turned towards me, some smiling, others blank, others annoyed.

'*Dui bu qi, dui bu qi*, excuse me,' I murmured. To distance myself from the eyes I counted them. On average there were 150 people per carriage, times six that made 900 people, times two, that made 1,800 eyes. To my relief, I found there was a free berth, but first I had the long return journey to get my pack. Another 1,800 eyes. Then back again, this time with my pack and its metal frame knocking into people and catching on the edge of seats: another 1,800 eyes, that made 5,400 eyes altogether. I reached the final carriage, close to tears, only to find that the door through to the exclusive hard sleeper was now locked. I banged but nobody came. I waited. The train stopped but still nobody came. Some boys came to help, shouting and thumping, but though people walked past, none of them took any notice. At last a guard released me to collapse on to my bunk, up on the top where no one could see me, stare at me, speak to me.

I lay awake most of the night, too exhausted to sleep, and listened to the train clattering into stations, to the voices of the guards calling to each other along the platforms, to the engines being changed. Sometimes I realised I was facing backwards, and that without my noticing we had changed direction. I loved travelling through the night, covering hundreds of unknown miles, the other passengers wrapped up in dark and in sleep secure that everything was taken care of. In all my journeys across China not one train was even a minute late. An elderly man crept in from hard seat and lay down on a narrow bunk beside his sleeping wife and grandchild; if the guards saw, they said nothing. Patrick and I had done the same ourselves.

By torchlight up on my top bunk I read Chinese reprints of English classics like *Lucky Jim* that had all the racier parts edited out, and I read translations of Chinese poetry and thought of Patrick, by now far away in Europe, far away from me.

My love is living
To the south of the Great Sea.
What shall I send to greet him?
Two pearls and a comb of tortoise shell:
I'll send them to him bound with ropes of jade.
They tell me he is not true;
They tell me he dashed my things to the ground,
Dashed them to the ground and burnt them
And scattered the ashes to the wind.
From this day to the ends of time
I must never think of him;
Never again think of him.

[First century AD]

I had written to him, but perhaps he did not want my letters. Where was he now? What was he doing? Who was he with?

Everyone was up and busy by 5 a.m., even before the loudspeakers. A twelve-year-old boy appeared on the opposite bunk and wanted to make friends. He babbled at me in

Chinese and was not in the least put off when I insisted I could not understand him. He persevered, and I discovered my Chinese had improved slightly. The main problem was that my geographical progress brought with it whole new ranges of accents and dialects, and even though Mandarin has been made the official national language, a Cantonese would find it hard to understand someone from Shanghai, or a Shanghai-ese to understand someone from Xian. Dialects change even from village to village. To me, the most curious accent was the national model, the Beijing accent, with its rolled 'r's' like the 'r's' of a West Country farmer. But I had built up a repertoire of phrases, some of which always worked, and some of which always failed. The latter I would try using every imaginable different tone, but never got any response. Being a tonal language, the number of homophones give rise to endless puns and, presumably, to endless jokes at the foreigner's expense.

The late-shift guards, still sleeping behind a curtained-off section, shouted angrily at us to be quiet, so we whispered for a while, but inevitably the noise crescendoed again. *'Yige, yige?'* the boy asked, holding up one finger. The word was passed down to his family on the lower bunks and to his father who perched on the window seat. They nodded. It is rare for women to travel alone. The father was a cadre in Taiyuan, and the mother, who had delicate, refined features and her hair in a bun, kept saying 'Newcastle.'

'Newcastle?'

'Hao, hao.'

It turned out that Newcastle had been twinned with Taiyuan, and the Newcastle councillors had just been to visit. They were distressed to hear I had seen nothing of this city of which they were so proud, and invited me to visit them next time I was there. When would that be, I wondered? In return for a chance to listen to my walkman, two boiled eggs appeared on my bed. I refused them – though these people were well-groomed with silk socks and smooth hair very different from their rough comrades in hard seat, they still had far less than I did. But soon a horribly sweet doughnut arrived and they would not hear of my refusal. I struggled through it, only to find another taking its place, my hand actually wrapped around it. I had nothing but the walkman to give in return, but in any case had never yet managed to persuade a Chinese person to accept anything. It was impossible to refuse their gifts, and impossible to make them accept mine.

– 11 –

Xian

At night I dreamt I was back in Changan;
I saw again the faces of old friends.
And in my dreams, under an April sky,
they led me by the hand to wander in the spring winds.
Together we came to the ward of Peace and Quiet;
We stopped our horses at the gate of Yuan Chen.

[Po Chui, 816 AD]

In just twenty-four hours I had travelled from winter into
spring, for here in Xian, once the ancient and splendid capital
Changan, the sun shone and the streets were lined with
yellow-green leaves and stalls selling cool drinks and ice
creams. There was a freshness here and I felt exultant and
lightfooted. Among some trees I was surprised by bird-song –
surprised because it was months since I had heard it last.
Hanging from the branches were dozens of cages of singing
birds. Squatting on their haunches beneath, taking the air,
chatting, smoking, were their elderly male owners. Even the
birds shared my mood.

Xian hoards one of China's great treasures, originally discovered by peasants digging a well in 1974, and one of the
world's most exciting archaeological finds: the Emperor Qin's
terracotta warriors. There are 6,000 of them, each with a
different facial expression, some ranged in rank and file, some
poised to shoot, others leading horses. They are huge, about

seven feet high, and were once painted green and yellow and red – but that was 2,300 years ago. Some are still unexcavated, and headless torsos and limbs are visible tossed about in a flood of sand. It was the Emperor Qin who ordered a previous cultural revolution, killing scholars and destroying all books and scrolls that he had not sanctioned; it was also he who united China and built the Great Wall by linking other smaller existing walls. He himself was buried beneath a mound close to his army, a mound still unexcavated but said to be a pleasure dome that Kublai Khan could never have rivalled, with gem-studded pavilions, mercury rivers, and the bodies of the artisans who were interred so their secrets should never be told.

I stayed in the People's Hotel, a mammoth Fifties palace surrounded by fountains and bridges, the 'people' being Western tour groups, overseas Chinese and, judging from the line-up of Red Flag and Shanghai limousines, an élite of Chinese cadres. Uniformed attendants did nothing more than open and close doors, and were bored and bad-tempered. I had surfaced into the 'outside world' of tourists who only the week before had been in LA, London or Sydney, and I quite enjoyed venturing out, if only for a moment. I met a Canadian woman teaching physics at the science institute in Beijing, the worst-equipped place she had ever seen, she said; I met an American professor here to advise the government on improving these science facilities; I met a Danish businessman maddened by the slowness of fixing up deals and exchanging contracts, and by the endless rounds of banquets; I met one Jimmy Jimbini, a lonely Walt Disney salesman in a red satin bomber jacket, desperate for a pick-up.

One day I was wandering through the Muslim quarter, a maze of tiny streets, searching for the Great Mosque. I met a diminutive and very old lady with a big camera on an embroidered strap also looking for the mosque. Together we found it, but it was closed for a few hours.

'I've left my tour group,' she confided and I liked her at once.

'I'm so bored of being shunted through Friendship Stores and Jade factories, being relieved of my foreign currency. I'm with an Italian group, all women with big rings on their fingers if you know what I mean.'

'Where are they now?'

'They've gone to see some ruins. I've got hours to myself!'

After we had walked a bit she tentatively asked if I ever ate street food.

'Yes, almost always. Why don't we go and have lunch together?'

'But don't you ever get ill?'

I reassured her, and gave her my own supposedly clean chopsticks, and we had bowls of *jaozi* in a tiny street café. She was enchanted, the dumplings so good, the sauce so spicy, and the price! Seven fen! (two pence). She was a remarkable woman who had worked for years in Africa as a midwife.

The mosque was opening as we arrived, the Muslims filing out from prayer, each man physically like the Han Chinese and dressed in usual Chinese clothes, but wearing small white skull caps. The priest had a white turban wrapped around his head. This Muslim community has existed here since Arab traders passed by on the silk route a thousand years ago. Having been suppressed during the Cultural Revolution, it is now allowed a certain amount of religious freedom by the new regime; the Chinese government is also not blind to the appeal both to tourists and to Arab investors whom they are trying to court.

Behind a bamboo curtain a few remaining worshippers were still bent over in prayer, their shoes left outside, so I did not go into the temple but wandered through the garden instead. Was it just the freshness of the day, or was it my mood? In any case, this mosque struck me as one of the loveliest places I had been to in China, even in Asia. Stupidly, I had expected round domes and a minaret and wailing mullah; instead – though there were some Arabic inscriptions – the buildings were Chinese pavilions set in a dreamy garden, bright green and pink and yellow. But it was less kitsch than most Chinese

Golmud to Lhasa, where 'demons rage, swine-headed, hairy skinned, with bulging eyes'.

The Potala, a cliff of stone, Lhasa.

Opposite above: Frenzy of prayer and prostration before the Jokhang Temple, the most revered in Tibet.

Opposite below: Prayer wheels, spinning messages up to the gods, line the Jokhang's inner courtyard.

Old man mumbling prayers; behind, cheap Chinese clothes are for sale.

Pilgrims dwarfed by Drepung buildings emerge from snow clouds.

Drepung Gompa, once the world's largest monastery, now houses less than three hundred monks.

Gyantse Gompa, a hive of shrines.

Pot bellied god, Gyantse.

gardens, less artificial; enclosed by a high wall, it seemed more like an Italian cloister, so delicate, so tranquil, so private.

One courtyard was completely given over to restoration, and a Muslim who spoke some English told me it was destroyed by the Chinese but was being rebuilt by the Muslim community with help from Muslims all over the world. It was a huge task, rebuilding a temple which, despite not having a roof or a floor had been in use until fairly recently. Signs still announced times of services and asked people to clean themselves thoroughly before entering.

I went to meet Irena's group and we all eyed each other with suspicion. These women with their big rings and thick make-up and overblown vulgarity were now far more foreign to me than the Chinese women in their shapeless monochrome shirts buttoned up to the collar, hanging over shapeless trousers; for all its ugliness I preferred the simple Chinese style. In return for my taking her to lunch, my new friend persuaded their driver to take me with them to the Confucius museum, to see the 'forest of steles', the 2,300 slate slabs inscribed with Confucian and other writings, as old as they are many. It was another beautiful place and I stayed for a long time, watching a man with a wadded cloth slapping ink on to steles to take rubbings of the calligraphy. Some of the calligraphy was engraved as a sweeping brushmark, a gloriously free abstract shape that had the added advantage of actually meaning something. A particularly flowing swoop said Happiness; the man saw how much I liked it and made a rubbing for me. He would accept nothing for it.

Another friend I made was an extraordinary Swiss German called Martin. We talked first in the hotel lobby where he was trying – unsuccessfully – to convince the receptionist he was a student. He had food between his teeth and mad cross-eyes and an accent so thick I thought he was Russian.

'I haf been vaiting four hours in zat ozer fuck-king hotel but zey refuse to gif me ze fuck-king bed,' he complained, his eyes fixed, I supposed on me. He was one of those travellers

determined to beat the system however great the effort, determined to wait for that bed he was sure was free. He always
knew where to get things cheap, how to pay RMB not 'Eff Eee
Cee'; if the authorities said you had to fly he always found a
route overland and always, as a matter of pride, travelled hard
seat not hard sleeper. Travelling was his profession, even his
life; he had no family and back in Switzerland stayed in a youth
hostel. He was one of the underworld of rootless people who
exist with a minimum of possessions and responsibilities by
making deals, buying and selling, smuggling, always moving on
through a world outside, though parallel to, the 'real world'. It
is a marvellously lawless society (but with its own codes of
conduct) that I had by now become part of. I felt a bond with
him in this tourist place.

Martin was a Marxist and admired the Chinese as much
as he despised the Indians. He argued that all religion is
oppressive, simply a weapon of dictators.

'All temples should be used as schools. Any improvement in
society can only come about with a revolution that wipes out
religion so all religion should be wiped out.' His cross-
eyes blazed. The main object of his loathing was the Dalai
Lama.

'The God-King!' he scoffed. 'Just a dictator with a self-
proclaimed right to rule and to keep society in a state of feudal
servitude. The best thing that ever happened to Tibet was
being liberated by the Chinese. Now everyone is equal, they
have schools and hospitals and new industries, and even a bath
house. I have heard that the Tibetans are the filthiest people on
earth, but now anyone who turns up to work stinking is sent
home and refused a day's pay.'

I was staggered. This was the first time I had heard the
Chinese line on Tibet.

'What do you know about it?' I was indignant.

'I've been told by someone who was in Tibet. He didn't like
it, and said it wasn't worth the effort of getting there.' It
was then that I finally made up my mind to go to Tibet. The

more Martin tried to dissuade me, the stronger grew my determination.

Tibet! Few names can conjure up more mystery, more magic, more strange harsh beauty than this. I heard it first when I was eight or nine years old and spent most of my time with my sisters trailing around in tattered ball gowns and dangerously spiked stilettos which were kept in an old laundry hamper that smelled of damp and tom-cats and moth-balls. As a special treat we were sometimes allowed to wear Red Indian outfits that were kept high up in a separate cupboard (where they are still) and which inspired new imaginary worlds. One day my mother lifted down these feathered head-dresses and brought out another flat box in which were fur hats and padded red coats and thick-soled embroidered boots.

My mother said her aunt had brought them back from Kalimpong in 1935 and that they were Tibetan. Tibet, she said, was a remote and dream-like place hidden behind the Himalayas, where monasteries clung to the snowy crags and monks performed mystic rituals. She said she had never been there, and now it was too late, everything had been destroyed by the Chinese. I had visions of Chinamen in hats like limpets scurrying around with fiendish knives chopping up Tibetans. The Red Indians were forgotten and for a while this became our new game.

Later I read Lobsang Rampa's *The Third Eye* which described these mystic rites, and the discovery of the true Dalai Lama which involved terrible testing hardships for the chosen child, starvation and freezing and an incision in the forehead which released the third eye and enabled him to see people's auras. It was only when I actually reached Tibet at last that I discovered Lobsang Rampa was a complete fraud who had invented it all, and was not a Tibetan lama but a Devon plumber.

Later still I was entranced by Heinrich Harrer's *Seven Years in Tibet*, and by *My journey to Lhasa* by Alexandra David-Neel, the stalwart Frenchwoman who disguised as a Tibetan, a Mongolian and a Ladakhi deceived the authorities successfully enough in the 1920s for her to break through their barriers and become the first Western woman to reach Lhasa. This was all I had read, but it was enough to know that Martin was wrong. I remembered the Tibetan family I had met in Nepal who had spoken sadly of their flight from the Chinese in 1959, and of 'home' which several of them had never seen. And now I was listening to Martin praising the Chinese and their destruction of more than 2,000 monasteries, the public humiliation and murder of monks, the imprisonment of thousands of Tibetans, the famine and starvation. Was this really necessary to improve the quality of Tibetan life? The only way I could answer that was by going to Tibet and seeing for myself.

But how was I to get there? It was too expensive to fly, and I did not want to risk altitude sickness, but more important, I wanted to go overland. The most convenient way overland was said to be by bus from Golmud, far out in the west of Qinghai province, but Golmud was officially closed to foreigners. I would have to travel by train for twenty-four hours to Xining and then another twenty-four hours to Golmud, only to face the possibility of being deported once I got there. Even if I was not deported I might find there was no bus after all. If there was a bus, I then faced a three- or four-day journey across deserts and rocks to Lhasa.

'Just imagine it,' Martin gloated, 'three or four days crammed into a rusted old bus with all the stinking Tibetans covered in fleas' (or 'flews' as he put it).

I laughed at him but could not help being secretly anxious. I began to have anxiety dreams from which I woke exhausted and which hung over me all day. Should I do it, and if so, how? Perhaps I would fly from Xian after all – it would save me having to fight for train tickets to Golmud.

'What!' Martin was incredulous. 'You can't mean you are going to spend 390 yuan on a plane ticket. That is twice what the Chinese pay. The authorities are milking you because they know foolish tourists will pay it.'

'Yes, I suppose you are right.'

'The bus costs only 70 yuan.'

'Does it.'

I spent the afternoon buying train tickets. Having tried to dissuade me from going to Tibet, Martin now became quite helpful and gave me some typed information which he had got hold of somehow. After a final dinner together we said farewell at the station and made a possible date to meet again and return to Europe on the trans-Siberian together.

'But furst I must get ze cheap roubles,' he said. 'Zey are cheapest on ze black market in Hong Kong. I vill go zere.'

– 12 –

Xining to Golmud

From Datong to Xian I had travelled from winter into spring; from Xian to Xining it was spring back to arid dusty winter. We soon left behind the lush green fields for desolate mountains and valleys hacked through by dried-up river beds like half-built motorways. The trees were still bare of leaves but when we reached Xining in late afternoon the next day the heat was intense, the dry industrial city sheltering under parched, dust-covered mountains. Even in the fairly short distance between the station and the hotel my lips cracked and my hair felt like straw.

The hotel was another Soviet block, a Russian-built monster with empty echoing corridors, and a lonely dusty bedroom for me. Over a solitary dinner I felt as if I was the only foreigner who had ever been or would ever want to come here.

But there are some attractions to Xining, one of which is Ta'ersi Lamasery, about an hour's bus ride outside the city. It was here that I had my first taste of Tibet, for what is now Qinghai province, of which Xining is the capital, was once a part of Tibet called Amdo, and was the birth place of the present Dalai Lama. What is now the Tibet Autonomous Region or Xizang province was simply south-west Tibet, and eastern Tibet, Kham, has been incorporated into Sichuan province.

Xining itself is a Chinese city, but there were small clutches of Tibetans strolling in the streets as well as Turkish-looking Uyigurs and Kazakhs from Xinjiang. Two Tibetan men, father and son, joined the bus to Ta'ersi, sweating in their hefty sheepskin coats tied up with pink sashes. They were very attractive with wide-apart slanting eyes and flashing gold teeth, and the Hans gazed at them. They fingered my jacket curiously, and laughed when I fingered their thick coats in return. If only we could speak!

'They no speak Chinese,' a young Han informed me. He, unfortunately, could speak a few words of English which he enjoyed saying, many times, looking at me for approval. I tried not to be rude – I don't suppose he had a chance to say his words very often. He was a worker in a watch factory, and his girl friend (very smart in flared jeans and high heels) was a doctor. Often in China I met this social mix of workers and more highly-qualified people. In Xian I had met a musician who had toured to Japan with his troupe; one of his brothers was studying composition in Beijing, and the other was a worker in a factory. People in China are proud of being workers.

It was the scent in the air that first told me we had arrived: incense, not the incense of Chinese joss sticks, but the delicious sweet smell of burning juniper wood and herbs. I felt lifted out of China and transported back to Nepal; memories came rushing in of the magical sanctuary at Muktinath and the two weeks I had walked to get there, crossing an 18,000 foot pass. It suddenly struck me that I had been travelling just as long to reach here, Ta'ersi, and though I had not known it, to return to a culture such as this had been my subconscious goal.

I longed to be alone here, to savour the atmosphere, to enjoy every detail, but my new friends had decided otherwise. Despite my protests they insisted on kindly paying for my entry and then hustling me from temple to temple, pointing out things, showing me what to photograph, never leaving me.

'Come along please,' the boy would order and sighing, trying to stay polite, I would go along. My irritation grew when each time we came before a Buddha the boy pretended to pray and then giggled and looked at me for applause. I hated his scoffing, and looked at the elderly Tibetan monks in their russet robes and wondered what horrors they had suffered at Chinese hands. Eventually the girl friend saw how sour-faced I had become, and took the boy away. It was time for me to leave China.

I had forgotten how rich Tibetan Buddhism is. In all the six temples every inch of space was smothered in fabrics: Buddhas and Bodhisattvas and other gods were draped with embroideries and *khatas*, the white silk prayer scarves, and illuminated by rows of yak butter candles in shallow silver dishes. Forests of pillars in the great dark halls were hung with carpets and weavings, some of Chinese dragons and others of Tibetan symbols. One elaborately painted courtyard was ringed by an upstairs balcony from which gazed stuffed animals: buffaloes, a goat, a bear, a deer. In the centre was an incense burner greased in yak butter and stuck all over with coins. In another, a tree just coming into leaf was hung with messages on paper and cloth, chinking lightly as the messages were wafted heavenwards on the breeze.

Monks were beating drums and chanting, while outside Tibetans were prostrating themselves, arms held up in prayer, then down they fell, foreheads pressed to the dust, then up again. Others were circling the temples clockwise, spinning the yards of prayer wheels that line the walls, spinning upwards the prayers wrapped inside. Some spun their own small hand prayer wheels and mumbled that hypnotic chant, '*Om mani padme hum*,' Oh Heavenly Jewel of the Lotus. The women had their hair tied in long thin plaits which were woven together at the bottom with false hair to form a sort of fan-shaped net down their backs. The heads of their children were shaved except for one tiny pigtail left pointing up into the air.

Nowhere could I find any information about Ta'ersi. It had clearly been a monastery of some magnificence, yet Alexandra David-Neel made no mention of it, and neither did Thubten Jigme Norbu, the Dalai Lama's brother, whose book *Tibet* I had got hold of. At the same time I was puzzled about the location of the great Kumbum monastery, the 'huge monastic town' where Alexandra David-Neel had lived, translating manuscripts, for two years in the early 1920s, and where, shortly after, Thubten Jigme Norbu was recognised as the reincarnation of the abbot, Tagtser. Maps and descriptions showed Kumbum to be somewhere near Xining, but no one I questioned had heard of it. I assumed the Chinese had destroyed it. Months later I discovered by chance that I had been in Kumbum all the time, for Ta'ersi and Kumbum were one and the same. Ta'ersi is its Chinese name, Kumbum its Tibetan.

So the tree I saw chinking with prayers was the offshoot of the famous tree, the miraculous engraved tree, that sprouted on the spot where the monastic reformer Tsong Khapa was born. Where his mother's blood flowed a tree is said to have grown, its leaves and bark engraved with a multitude of holy images and words. Even the French priest, Abbé Huc, who saw the tree in the mid-nineteenth century, was amazed. These images, he declared, grew naturally on the leaves and trunk. 'Kumbum' means 'Hundred thousand images'.

Tsong Khapa dedicated his life to reforming the monasteries, cleansing them of dubious tantric practices, stressing celibacy and study, and founding the 'Yellow Hat' or Gelukpa sect of which the Dalai Lama is the head. Here at Kumbum centuries later, Alexandra David-Neel listened to the monks' orchestras greeting the dawn, shared in their meals of soup and tea, and stayed perhaps in one of the buildings now converted into a primitive guest house. She was the first woman allowed to stay in a monastery; normally women left at sundown. The year she was there, Thubten Jigme Norbu was born. Aged eight he was enthroned as abbot, rather to his own surprise. The living he inherited was wealthy enough to support not only the hundreds of monks at Kumbum, but three other monasteries as well.

How things had changed; the Red Guards had wreaked their usual havoc. Temples were being restored however, and there are three little hotels, so this is clearly intended to become a major tourist site. Many stalls leading up to the monastery sell Tibetan silver, weavings and other handicrafts, but as yet these are mostly for pilgrims and monks, and Tibetans trading furs – fox, leopard, and others I did not recognise.

Having intended to stay there, I felt suddenly saturated and in a fever to leave, to leave Kumbum, to leave Xining, to leave China. I suddenly could not face going on to Tibet. I had seen all I wanted to see, this was enough: I could not go on looking and looking. I ran down hill to find a bus, impatient to get away as soon as possible, to return to Beijing and take the trans-Siberian back to Europe. I wanted to run for home. All my ideals about single-mindedness and being committed to every action were forgotten. Instead I was awash with doubts and self-contradictions. But next to me on the bus was an old Tibetan swilling his evil-smelling *chang* and mumbling his prayers at the same time; he smiled at me, and I knew that my fate – or karma – was decided, and that I would head on west after all.

Back in the pocket of Xining the heat was burning, and I punctuated my progress down the streets and through the market with stops at water-ice stalls along the way. The market stretched over several streets, but the only vegetable on sale looked like grass – perhaps chives. Otherwise it was mostly noodles, *jaozi* and *baozi*, and the round steamed buns, grey and damp, called *mazous*. I was pushed aside by two boys who dragged another along the street, holding him up under the arms with his feet thudding along behind, his knees flopping from side to side. He must have been dead, or dead drunk, or suffering a kind of fit, but no one took any notice. They were much more interested in me, chirruping 'Hello, hello,' every few seconds which at first was friendly and soon became irritating.

Xining's most prosperous person must be the hairdresser. Nowhere had I seen such elaborate styles. Most Chinese women wear their hair tied back in bunches or plaits, or else cut short and permed, but here women had long hair which was parted severely down the back, short and curled on top, the long hair beneath rolled into two long ringlets which were tied at the bottom with red bows. They could not rival the Tibetan women, but these girls were very fancy.

I wanted a map of Xining, but the China International Travel Service (CITS) cupboard in the hotel was locked and the man with the key had gone to Tibet. But I talked to the handsome young man there and discovered there was a weekly flight from Golmud to Lhasa leaving in two days. I did not intend to fly, but I was now in the hands of the fates, and if they had decided I should fly, then I must give them the opportunity to have their way. That meant I would have to leave Xining tonight. So, armed with a letter from this man stating that I had to catch a plane from Golmud, I rushed to the station and was given a ticket for tonight's train which only that morning I had been refused. It was now 29 April, and I had been told there were no seats on this train until 13 May. It was often like this in China. For no apparent reason a ticket seller, hotel reception-ist, or shop assistant would say, '*Meiyou, Meiyou*', meaning no, nothing, go away I can't be bothered, it's for Chinese only; and there was nothing one could do.

Winding round the platform and out into the forecourt, inching towards the train, was a queue, and I was at the back. I had before me the prospect of standing in the train for twenty-four hours. But I felt a rap on my shoulder and turned to see a guard demanding sharply to see my passport and travel permit. He studied them closely and told me to follow him. Everything was over; he was not going to let me on the train, and I would have to find another route to Lhasa. I tried to remember that every action is a thing important in itself, but it was difficult under these circumstances to see the importance of coming all the way here just to be turned away. I followed him into an office. He disappeared, taking my documents with him. The train was leaving in three minutes. I walked into a neighbouring office to find him showing my travel permit to another official. They handed it back to me, and pointed to 'Means of Transportation'. I had not noticed before, but 'car' (meaning bus or truck) had been crossed out. Then I remembered the note the CITS man had written. I produced it, looking as nonchalant and confident as I could, and it worked. I was rushed out of the office and on to the train, not to the back of the queue for hard seat, but to the luxurious soft sleeper class. The guard said something to the girl attendant, and I was shown into a panelled compartment, the door shut. The train left.

I sank back into the soft pillows, turned off the loud speaker, switched on the tasselled table lamp, and poured myself a cup of tea in the blue and white lidded cups with which China's élite are provided. Everything was going to be all right – the only problem would be paying for this unasked for luxury.

We drew out of the city into dry terraced valleys, layer upon receding layer built up over thousands of years to prevent erosion. Green shoots of millet were beginning to appear above the yellow soil. We passed Lake Qinghai, large and saline, and isolated villages towered over by rocky mountains. On their peaks I glimpsed prayer flags fluttering from bundles of sticks. Who had put them there, these mysterious reminders of the gods and spirits of the Tibetan world?

I thought of Thubten Jigme Norbu who, with a vast caravan of servants and thousands of animals, had come this way on foot, walking to Lhasa in order to complete his studies at one of the great state monasteries. The journey took him three months. The distance is over a thousand miles, and pilgrims are said to have covered it by prostrating themselves, measuring out their lengths on the ground.

Periodically train guards came in to look at the travel permit and the letter, and without saying anything handed them back. I opened my door to see the view on both sides of the train, but they kept shutting it as if they wanted to keep me out of sight. Word got out however and I was soon joined by workers who sat down beside me on the beds: my brief solitude was over. I unfolded my map to show them where I had been, and as I named a place so they repeated it after me in unison until it became a sort of litany: Hong Kong, Guangzhou, Zhanjiang, Hainan, Shanghai, Suzhou, Nanjing, Beijing, Datong, Xian, Xining. When I mentioned Lhasa, their reaction was like that of all the Chinese I had met: surprise that I should want to go to such a backward place, and horror at the prospect of such a journey.

'*San tien, si tien*, three or four days!' The guard returned to shoo them all away and to lead me down the passage to a cheaper hard sleeper where I was to stay. Sitting on my bed were a group of men passing round a bottle of spirits, getting rapidly drunk, and playing their favourite game which involves shouting out numbers '*liu, liu, ba, jiu*' and making the appropriate hand signals. One, with pebble glasses, sat heavily on my knees and thrust the bottle at me; his friend was already snoring on someone else's bunk.

I was rescued by an imperious deputation from the dining car who had come to escort me to dinner. There was silence when I entered and everyone looked up from their bowls of soup. I was shown to a seat and a waitress bustled up with a napkin and chopsticks; I felt all eyes on me as I wielded them and prayed I would not drop anything.

I woke to find the landscape had plateaued out to desert, not Sahara-type dunes but mile upon mile of rocks sprinkled with a layer of sand, and occasional mountain ranges opening into limitless tundra that stretched in a great circle all round us, nothing growing but the odd scraggy bush bouncing about in the wind. The rivers had withered to tiny streams or disappeared altogether in the rubble.

O Soul go not to the West
Where level wastes of sand stretch on and on;
And demons rage, swine-headed, hairy-skinned,
With bulging eyes;

– 141 –

Who in wild laughter gnash projecting fangs.
O Soul go not to the West
Where many perils wait!

[Anon second or third century BC]

It seemed like the edge of the world, a forgotten deserted place. We passed ruined villages where all that remained were the husks of houses, outer walls crumbling back into the sand from where they came. Some were nomad villages, others more substantial with vestiges of grand gates and the red gleam of a Chinese star. Qinghai is China's Siberia, populated mostly by convicts in labour reform camps; millions have been imprisoned here since the Revolution, many on trumped-up charges and many, even today, imprisoned without trial. Most of the convicts never return home after being released and it is they who live in the few meagre settlements that lie alongside the railway line. Peasant women from poor rural villages are sometimes offered incentives to come here to marry and settle.

It was only on this journey that I came to appreciate the vastness of China. I had travelled more than one thousand miles since Beijing, and I felt an intimation of infinity as I pressed onwards across the earth, thrilling after eastern and southern China where almost every inch is cultivated or inhabited. But I also saw the enormity of China's problem: so much of its space is completely unproductive and uninhabitable. The railway line across it, which will eventually penetrate to the heart of Tibet, is a momentous feat, cutting into the sides of mountains and breaking in and out of tunnels.

Yet even here there were small touches of humanity. One family were leaving the train with boxes of potted plants, so green and fertile, a bizarre sight and a touching one too as these people attempt to make their home more bearable.

At last we reached the end of the line: Golmud. Here civilisation peters out. What is this town doing here in the desert with its freezing winters and hot, hot summers? There is a strong military presence and perhaps other people here work with the oil and mineral deposits said to exist. It must be a miserable place of exile.

A girl on the train had laughed when I asked if there was a hotel. I tried again at the station and approached a soldier to ask (in Chinese) for the *zhaodaisuo*, whereupon he jumped back in alarm and stuttered that he only spoke Chinese. I tried *binguan*, and another's eyes lit up and he pointed to a bus. So there was somewhere to stay: that was the first problem over.

We drove past desolate six-storey flats to the hotel, from where I was sent to the Public Security Bureau, the police. I had no idea what they would do with me. Not only was I in a closed place, but I was also intending to travel illegally over-land. In the last resort I could produce that useful letter from CITS, which would explain what I was doing here, but that would mean I would have to fly after all. Perhaps I was fated to fly: I was not sure. Public Security was a collection of whitewashed buildings in a walled compound, and as I arrived, so did the official on her bicycle. She was delighted to hear I was English, for she herself had been an English teacher here in Golmud. Far from deporting me, she told me that there was a daily bus to Lhasa, and then took me to the bus station herself. Before leaving, she urged me to stay in Golmud for another day as tomorrow was May Day and there was to be a celebration basket ball match.

My relief and happiness vanished when I saw the bus which confirmed my worst fears. It stood in a yard like a tired old cart-horse, a battered hulk crumbly with rust and missing most of its windows. A man in the office was adamant that this really was the bus to Lhasa; I could not believe this machine could even move out of the yard, let alone over a 15,000-foot pass.

'Yes,' he insisted, 'this is the bus, and it is leaving tomorrow at 4 a.m.'

'How long is the journey?'

'Two days.'

'Only two days?' my heart lifted a little. 'But how can it be so quick?'

'Because there are no stops.'

My heart sank again. That meant no resting at night, just continuous driving, continuous discomfort for forty-eight hours. Up so high in this clear climate the cold at night would be severe. I did not book a seat immediately; perhaps I was intended to fly after all. But how could I know? I had no fortune teller with me. Only I could see the signs, and interpret them. I made a deal. If I could pay for my hotel in RMB then it meant I would take the plane; if I had to pay in FEC I would go by bus. Without arguing, I paid in FEC.

I watched the basket ball match (the girl from Public Security was playing) and looked at a couple of moth-eaten Bactrian camels with sagging humps. There was nothing much else to do. I did buy myself a large blue padded jacket with a fake fur collar, the kind that everyone wears, in the hope that this would keep me warm in the bus; and a few bars of Lucky chocolate as my supplies. But I remembered the repeated stops for food between Guangzhou and Hainan, and later gave the chocolate to a child.

Now that the moment had come, I could hardly wait to leave for Tibet. I had travelled thousands of miles over many months and yet the people here looked the same as all the others, wore the same grey and blue clothes, sold exactly the same things in their shops, all displayed in the same way. The street names were the same, the buildings the same, even the piped music crackling through the loudspeakers at every street corner was the same. Yet one day I was in tropical Hainan, next in the brisk cold of Shanghai, then in the showery spring of Xian, and then in the parched heat of Golmud. Here in Golmud the sun still blazed at nine o'clock at night, while east in Beijing it was dark by five o'clock. In this vast country where Qinghai alone is the size of France, I marvelled at the success of the Party in spreading out its tentacles.

– 13 –

Golmud to Lhasa

I lay awake for most of that night so had no need of my alarm. As the electricity was off I dressed by torchlight and crept down the dark passage and out into the street. There was no moon, and swirling dust blew up into my face as I beat my way against the wind, head ducked, to the bus station. It was deserted. Then in snatches some Tibetans arrived, grinning their gold and false teeth smiles, and stinking of the uncured sheepskin that lined their coats. They helped me to heave my pack up on to the roof and lash it down under a tarpaulin, by which time the Chinese passengers had arrived and were fighting their way to the seats. The bus was, of course, packed, the Tibetans filling the back rows.

Our road out of Golmud soon disintegrated into a dirt track and then dwindled altogether. My map marked a road to Lhasa, but it was a lie! There was no such thing. It was still being built. As the driver swerved to avoid the piles of rocks and sand that blocked our way, we hurtled along, careering down steep banks, swaying from side to side, suddenly jolting to a stop. The Tibetans smashed their heads against the roof, but smiled all the time. Several times I was really afraid: I knew this journey would be long and arduous, but I never expected it to be perilous too, and I tried to work out ways of saving myself if we crashed over.

After eight or nine hours the driver abruptly, and for no obvious reason, left the track to veer off across the scrub and dunes. A long way ahead was an outcrop of what appeared to be stationary trucks, and as we joined them so our bus also sank into deep sand and mud. It was a graveyard of abandoned and half-unloaded trucks, some of which had been here a long time, judging from their decaying state. We all climbed out to push the bus while the driver revved the engine and pumped out black smoke. Nothing happened.

I wandered away and climbed a sandbank, and there at the top I saw mile upon mile upon mile of flat golden grassland, an immense tableland empty of any single feature, but ringed on the distant horizon by a tiny line of glittering saw-toothed peaks, the Kunlun range that divides Tibet from Xinjiang in a great east-west prong. As I stood before this desert of grass I found it hard to comprehend how much of this planet is so totally empty. Perhaps this was the *Chang thang* where Alexandra David-Neel saw for the first time the *lung gompa*, the feat of psychic travelling, when she glimpsed in the distance a man leaping across the plateau at superhuman speed. Coming up from Kumbum, this was the first human being she had seen for ten days.

Somehow the bus was freed, and we returned to the track leaving behind other less fortunate drivers. A team of workers in PLA khaki flagged us down, and there followed much shouting between them and our driver, the passengers joining in to yell abuse. The gang was refusing to let us pass, and I was told to get off the bus. Perhaps they were not allowing the bus to continue with me – illegally – on board. Perhaps I was going to be abandoned. I climbed slowly down the steps, dreading the worst, and found myself face to face with the leader of the gang, a bald thug. What was I supposed to do? I asked him if he spoke English. He said No, and looked rather sheepish, and at that moment a man from our bus pushed past me, grabbed the thug by the lapels, and shoved him out of the way. Miraculously we were suddenly allowed to pass. He had been shamed in front of a foreigner.

This brave passenger was one of three who spent the journey sitting up on the engine at the front, all wearing trench coats with upturned collars, stetsons and shades. One even smoked a cheroot, and for most of the journey they played poker, straight out of Chicago 1935. Sitting behind me was a peasant couple of the roughest sort, the woman with a filthy strip of cloth wrapped around her head. She slept for most of the time in agonising-looking positions, her head flopping back behind her seat and knocking against the metal bar, her mouth wide open. Whatever she ate, she vomited.

We had left Golmud at 4 a.m. and did not stop for breakfast until 2.30 p.m. ten and a half hours later, by which time I was almost faint with hunger. Everyone but me had brought bundles of cakes and biscuits and tins of mandarin oranges which they ate with chopsticks, but I had nothing. I thought with regret of that Lucky chocolate. I had not even brought any water, and was rapidly dehydrating in the parched dusty air. At last we passed some shacks and the driver was shouted at and pleaded with to stop. It was a desolate place where truckdrivers sleep and eat and refuel. We found a grimy back room behind a coal shed and a man in a greasy apron to cook omelettes for us on an open fire.

As it grew dark again people tried to sleep, slumped over each other, heads banging against the metal bar in front. After the sun dropped the cold intensified, though I was snug if immobile with innumerable layers beneath my jacket. We were all so well padded against the cold that there was not enough room on the seats, so for forty-eight hours I had to cling on to stop myself being pushed into the aisle into which everyone was, of course, spitting. There was no way to get comfortable. I had given a spare pair of trousers to my neighbour to fold against the window as a pillow, and in return he gave me his shoulder which he patted invitingly. But he was so small and his shoulder so low down that I could not reach it without doubling up and giving myself terrible neck ache. I tried every possible position: my head on my arms knocking against the bar in front, my body twisted round with my head resting on the bar behind, but they were all agony.

Late at night, around midnight, we stopped for the second time. To try and sleep I had taken out my contact lenses and emerged in a myopic haze from the cocoon of the dark bus into a smoky room where I drank a bowl of sooty boiled water, sitting on a wooden stool under pictures of men on horseback. They were lit by the sickly sputter of a paraffin lamp and by a wild coal fire over which three men were boiling soup and steaming *mazous*. I returned to the bus to find my little neighbour had kindly bought me a *mazou*, grey and damp. I put it discreetly in my bag.

Time toiled on and I welcomed the first pallid glimmers of dawn with relief. There were signs of life outside: soldiers in Chinese fur hats with the ear flaps down emerging from tents and stamping their feet in the cold before brewing tea on a gas burner. Soldiers and convicts are building the road and the railway line; the cost of civilian labour for this monumental task would have been more than China could afford. Then, at about 7 a.m., we climbed up and up above a wide brown valley, up to 15,000 feet over the Tanggula Pass, and there before me was Tibet! Before me was the land of mystics and hermits who live walled up in caves, incarcerated in the mountainside, the land of demons and omens, of *gompas* and *dubthabs*, of pilgrims and nomads, the Land of Snows. Black shapes moved across the ochre grass that grew sporadically on the mountainside, and fleetingly but as though on cue, I saw my first yaks. Nesting in hollows beneath peaks were villages, compounds clad in dried mud the pale brown colour of the earth and grass, striped with whitewash and topped by a flurry of ragged pennants fluttering prayers up to the gods. I sent up my own prayer of thanks for my safe arrival, and for the end to those weeks of anxiety and indecision and discomfort that had at last brought me here.

We had crossed the sources and streams of three of the world's greatest rivers, the Yangtze, the Mekong and the Salween. Over in western Tibet is the source of the Indus, and we were heading south towards the Brahmaputra, known in Tibetan as the Tsangpo, which flows out into the Bay of

Bengal. The watershed of the world! Three months earlier I had been on a boat in the mouth of the Yangtze where it was so wide the opposite bank had disappeared off the horizon. Three months before that I had sat by the bank of the Mekong looking across at Laos and Burma; and before that I had rowed along the Brahmaputra in Bangladesh. How little had I imagined I would see these rivers again.

At midday we stopped in our first Tibetan town, Nagqu, a market town dominated at its crossroads by a fortress-like building with high slanting whitewashed walls and window-surrounds painted black and topped with red flowers. It was the same shape as monasteries in Ladakh, built strong to withstand not armies but the months of bleak icy windswept weather. It was now May – spring – but purplish snow clouds hung dangerously low, about to offload, and I was glad to shelter by the fire inside a café in this building and drink a bowl of hot soup.

In the streets strutted Tibetans in sienna-red coats lined with every sort of animal fur and hung with swords and daggers, both men and women with their hair tied into long plaits threaded with red or blue wool, then twisted round their heads. Their feet were encased in the embroidered wedge-soled boots that I recognised at once. Never have I seen such powerful and dignified people, the women like squaws with burnt red-brown faces and white teeth, their cheekbones high and eyes slanting. There is a story that hundreds of years ago some Tibetans went so far north they had to go south again, perhaps crossing the Bering Straits, and that this is the origin of the American Indians. Certainly the similarity is extraordinary. Many of these people buying and selling in the market were Khampas, the fierce bandit-traders who come from eastern Tibet to trade throughout the country. Once nomads feared for their lives if Khampas approached their tents; it was they who initiated the rebellion against Chinese suzerainty in 1959 which, despite their brave efforts, failed and led to the total annexation of Tibet into China. The Chinese argue that

Tibet was always part of China, but looking round today there was no way I could believe that Tibet was anything other than a foreign-occupied country. These people racially have nothing in common with the Chinese.

The town looked poor. There was nothing much for sale but meat in the back of a cart which people picked up to inspect, and dropped in disgust. Otherwise there were only hard-boiled eggs, sweets, Tibetan clothes, and the usual Chinese khaki trousers and little black shoes. A dog was decomposing in the river. Dogs! How long was it since I had seen a dog? They had all been eaten in China. There were plenty here, fearsome scraggy brutes, but here none the less. It is fundamental to Tibetan Buddhists not to kill any living creature, for that creature may well be a reincarnation of some fellow being, though how much this rule is obeyed today is hard to tell. In the past it was only the Muslims in Tibet who killed animals for meat, though the Tibetans ate it.

We waited in Nagqu for several hours while our bus was fiddled with from underneath. It was the first of many break-downs that day, particularly frustrating now we were so close to Lhasa. Then, as promised, the clouds unleashed thick curtains of snow which blew through the broken windows into the bus itself. The windscreen wipers had collapsed so someone operated them manually. But the sun broke through in time to dodge between the Gyade mountains and subside in pink and orange glory. Then it was down again, south into the Lhasa valley, the valley of the Kyichu river. At last, at midnight, we turned into a town and the Tibetans on the back seat cheered: it was Lhasa, and there, its white walls glinting as it clung to its rock and towered above the city, a cliff of stone, was the Dalai Lama's mighty palace, the Potala.

– Part III –

– 14 –

Lhasa at last

I struggled stiffly out of the bus, retrieved my dust-encrusted pack, and promptly got a nose bleed. I had been expecting it: Lhasa stands at 13,000 feet and the air is thin and dry. So it was a muffled goodbye I bid to my fellow passengers, most of whom were laughing and chattering in their excitement to be home. I left them and trying to quench the flow and carry my bags at the same time, staggered off through the dark streets. Keeping the Potala firmly on my right, I headed for what I supposed to be the centre of the city, but all I found were building sites and concrete system-built office blocks. These avenues were as wide and as blank, the buildings as ugly, and the distances between them as stretched as in every other Chinese town: I felt a deepening anticlimax. Perhaps I had come all this way to find nothing of Lhasa was left. Perhaps the Chinese had destroyed everything. Perhaps the Potala was just a hollow shell. Snow began to pierce my face and hands in freezing little darts; a stray cur barked viciously and then scuttled away; a couple of men flitted past under the streetlight but ignored my attempts to ask them the way; my pack was slipping down my back and my nose was bleeding harder than ever: I could go no further. Then a man appeared from the shadows and without my asking, or him saying anything, led me to the guest-house. In the sleep-filled dormitory a middle-aged woman breathed oxygen from a pillow bag. She had flown in from Chengdu, her daughter whispered, and was suffering from altitude sickness;

her body had swollen and she was kept awake by the deafening pounding of her heart.

We were woken early by the blare of Chinese music and the chattering of women, men shouting orders and the chink chink of breaking stones. Lhasa was being rebuilt. The area round the guest-house was a turmoil of noise and motion from early morning until night, with women chipping stones, humping them on their backs up wooden stairs to the builders, the radio doing its best to spur them on. Preparations were under way for the planned tourist onslaught, and on the edge of the city a 1,200-bed hotel and shopping complex was nearing completion. The Chinese invasion, the Cultural Revolution, and now mass tourism: I was afraid of what I would find – or not find – when I went outside. I dreaded being disappointed and hardly dared go downstairs, so I walked over to the flat roof opposite my room and looked out.

Up above the city my excitement returned. Lhasa! Tibet! The Himalayas! It was hard to believe I was here. Even if nothing of the old life remained, it was enough just to have arrived, and to breathe this clear air and to sniff the sweet mingling of incense and dung.

All around me was a necklace of burnt-umber mountains drifting in and out of the thick brown shrouds of snow clouds. Neatly contained within them lay the city of Lhasa, the mud roofs, tin roofs, dirt tracks, asphalt, and rising straight up from the flat valley the twin hills, one crowned by the Potala, its zigzag paths twisting up towards secular white wings and sacred red centre. It was in the centre that the Dalai Lama lived. Miraculously the Potala was saved from the destruction of the last thirty years; the other hill, Chagpori, was less fortunate. Once the Tibetan College of Medicine stood at its top: now nothing remains. At the other end of the city, close to my rooftop, rose the elegant golden layers and curves and peaks and arcs of the Jokhang, the most ancient temple in Tibet, and perhaps the most revered. It is the focus of pilgrimages from all over the country, from beyond mountain ranges and forests, pilgrimages once made on foot. I glanced below me and there were the mud-rutted lanes that surround the temple: this was the Lhasa I had come to see.

Full of renewed energy, I ran downstairs and out into the wide Chinese street lined with new buildings but designed with at least some concession to Tibetan style, with the whitewashed walls and black window-surrounds I had seen in Nagqu. Cobblers had laid out their tools on sheets along the pavement. Behind them, opening off the main street, was a stinking passageway, and this I followed beneath the severe façades and dark narrow windows of old Tibetan houses, their thick walls (unlike the new versions) sloping outwards to let light penetrate the alley. I picked my way along a quagmire of mud, broken paving stones and excrement, and through doorways glimpsed scruffy courtyards and sodden straw, a tethered cow, a ragged snot-caked child, an old woman sitting in a pool of sun. The passage led to a wider lane which in turn opened out into a small square, the market. Long wooden tables bent under the weight of hairy yak skins packed with sun-yellow rancid yak butter which was sliced with a wire and weighed. Heavy glass jars held firm yak yoghurt which I had for breakfast that day and from then on; there were hunks of meat too, and the green grass-like vegetable I had seen in Xining.

Four or five old men were sitting on footstools round a thermos; they saw me looking at them and waved me over. They were drinking a sickly yellow-grey fluid, hot, with pimples of fat bobbing on the surface.

Yak butter tea. They pressed me to try some, so I did, and found it was not only greasy but salty. They laughed at my disgust, but if I convinced myself it was soup, not tea, it was just bearable. Later, a Chinese doctor prescribed butter tea as a cure for the nose bleeds. The grease, he said, would counteract the dryness of the air which caused them. I could not bring myself to follow his advice.

A few yards further on I found what I was looking for: the Barkhor. The Jokhang temple is like a drop in a pool, encircled by concentric rings. On the outskirts of Lhasa was Lingkhor, once a five-mile-long pilgrimage, now a main road. Within that comes the Barkhor, the social centre, the trading centre, and the pilgrims' centre of Lhasa. Around the circular street Tibetans stroll clockwise from morning to night. It is the meeting place for girls whose thick-soled red felt boots poke out from under coarse woollen maroon coats or grey-blue shift dresses which are clasped at the waist with elaborate copper buckles. They wear long striped aprons and their waist-length black hair is threaded with turquoise and coral, their necks hung with ropes of rough-cut beads. Other girls from different parts of Tibet wear shorter belted sleeveless tunics, and their hair is piled up under golden pillbox hats. Many are astonishingly beautiful and elegant.

Equally handsome were the swaggering Khampa men, many over six feet tall, wrapped in coats or *tubas*. Riding precariously on their heads above plaited hair were green felt hats, a cross between stetsons and bowlers, and jewels dangled from their ears. These swashbucklers stood together in clusters, trading swords, chunky amber, turquoise and coral which they produced from the folds of their coats. Several tried to sell me their treasures, and girls offered me necklaces and jewel-studded metal *gahus* or reliquaries which they themselves were wearing. Tibetans are famous traders and notoriously hard bargainers, but I did not want to buy anything, and they did not persist. Take it or leave it, they seemed to say, and I always suspected they were laughing to themselves.

Lining the Barkhor were stalls under orange awnings, and tunnel-like shops selling strips of multi-coloured woven fabric, *tubas* and dresses, boots and belts; mats laid on the ground displayed antiques and trinkets, copper pots and tea urns, jugs, bowls, strings of prayer beads, old coins, photos of the Dalai Lama. Some stalls sold wood-block printed prayers; others were hung with *thangkas*, the prayer banners painted with religious scenes and mandalas; and hand-woven carpets. Incense billowed from an immense free-standing chimney; since earliest Bon – pre-Buddhist – times, juniper was considered delicious and nourishing for the *Tisas*, the demigods who feed on smells.

Among strollers and shoppers were pilgrims who, as in Kumbum, swung prayer wheels and murmured the *ngag*, the six sacred symbols of Tibetan Buddhism, *Om mani padme hum*, working their beads like rosaries. Some sat on the road in front of *thangkas*, chanting prayers and collecting money for their pains. One old man was dressed in a scarlet spotted jacket and a red cap which tapered to a point at the crown and flapped up at the sides – it was a hat, I read, of someone 'skilled in the art of meditation'. Every day he sat cross-legged in the street, his pot steadily filling with alms. Others were prostrating themselves, one man gripping two wooden blocks which clattered as he flung himself to the ground, the force of his body sliding him towards the temple. Another man had strips of rubber tyre strapped round his hands and knee – he had only one leg. Yet he fell forward and heaved himself up, forward and up, measuring out his own length as he worked his painful pilgrimage. A team of seven boys, naked to the waist, stretched up their arms in unison then drew them down in front of their foreheads, mouths and hearts, and fell to the ground, their hands clasped in prayer over their heads, foreheads pressed into the dirt. Then they pushed up and jumped one step to the side, progressing sideways, slowly, following the command of the largest boy whose eyes stared with fanaticism. Their foreheads and elbows and bellies were grey with dust.

At the entrance to the Jokhang the pilgrims collected in a frenzy of prostration that continued late into the night. Men and women turned down their coats to the waist to keep cool in their exertions, and tied the bottoms with string. Out of respect for the Buddha, their feet were bare, and hats were hung on the red temple pillars. Some fell on to mats, others directly on to the paving; over the centuries their bodies have smoothed out their shapes on the stones.

The Jokhang is the St Peter's of Tibetan Buddhism, and was

the first temple to be built in Tibet, nearly 1,400 years ago. The seventh century king Strontsan Gampo was a Bonpoba, a believer in spirits and shamans – an animist. But he married a devout Buddhist, Princess Bhrikuti of Nepal, and was converted to the Buddhist faith; the temple was built to house the holy images she brought with her. Strontsan Gampo made a second political marriage, to the Tang dynasty princess Wong Shen Konjo, and she too brought a revered image of Siddhartha Gautama before he became a Buddha that remains in the temple still. The Jokhang, the 'House of the Lord', was designed and built by Nepalese craftsmen, but legend tells of mysterious trouble with the foundations, and the temple kept collapsing. The secret was known by an old man in the east who accidentally revealed that a mighty lake lay beneath, and as he told the secret, so a great rumbling was heard and a lake bubbled up out of the ground, drowning him and everyone around, but leaving Lhasa free.

From then on the foundations stood firm. The lake was Koko Nor, also known as Lake Qinghai, and I, ignorant of the story, had sped past it in the train from Xining to Golmud.

The entrance is marked by two huge prayer wheels spun morning and night, and two giant demons seated astride dragons, clutching in their hands serpents and rats – fearsome enough to scare off any evil spirit though not, it seems, the Chinese. Until recently the temple was closed to Tibetans and used by the Chinese as a dormitory and cinema. It is hard to imagine it now, looking at the exquisite glossy wall paintings of the thousand Buddhas carefully protected behind wire netting, but almost everything in the temple has been restored. A nun with a shaved head was sculpting a clay mould for a Buddha's head and behind her stood the almost completed statue. Soon the scars will be hidden and the world will wonder what the fuss was about.

But perhaps under the new more liberal regime the Tibetans are getting their revenge. I entered the temple with a small gaggle of Chinese who, unlike the Tibetans, did not remove their caps. Within minutes a large and forbidding monk swathed in russet robes bore down and expelled them.

Between the outer walls and the inner sanctum is another clockwise pilgrimage, repeating the Barkhor outside. This is measured out by three walls of elaborately carved prayer wheels two feet high, each one sent whizzing round by the faithful as they passed. The inner sanctum is the fourth and narrowest circle. Tibetans had squeezed into a long queue that filed slowly and patiently round the dark temple, each pilgrim entering every small shrine to touch their foreheads against a holy relic and to drip offerings of yak butter into the flickering rows of candles. The air was thick with the smell of burning butter and incense, and with the ceaseless droning of prayers. Even the swaggering Khampas had let down their plaits and stood with humbly bowed heads before the images. An excited man led me by the hand to a spot behind an altar whispering, 'Dalai Lama, Dalai Lama!' and pointed to the ground. A small footprint – that of a child – was pressed into it.

I left the temple and wandered across the building site to the Chinese town. Until 1959 this area was covered by woods and a lake where in summer people set up tents and had picnics. The distance of the town from the Potala was a respectful one and served to emphasise its grandeur and sanctity. This is where the Chinese chose to build. Around the Jokhang I had seen almost no Chinese; here I saw hardly any Tibetans. The few pilgrims who strolled along the wide streets looked in at the department stores with almost as much curiosity as I. These were two separate towns for two separate races, one the conqueror, the other the conquered. I could not help noticing that the Chinese here walked with a new swagger and laughed louder than they would in the rest of China; they lolled about in the Chinese No. 1 Guest-House with the arrogant ease of the colonial official. Tibet is considered a hardship post, but to be master is one of the attractions, and to make the Chinese feel at home, shops are stocked with tins of pork, tea, and the other familiar Chinese goods. In the bookshop was a huge portrait of

Chairman Mao: either they are behind the times here, or else Mao was forced on the people so much more vigorously and successfully than in the rest of China, that his removal takes longer.

From that first day, these were my haunts, the Tibetan city for the 'real' Lhasa, the Chinese city for the shower. There was no running water at Snowlands Guest-House, and though we were given thermoses of hot water and enamel basins for washing (the slops tipped down a chute into the courtyard) six people in each dormitory did not allow for any privacy. The bath-house was steamy with quantities of hot water under which I basked. We wore wooden clogs, as in a Turkish *hamam*, and Tibetan, Chinese and English, we all stared curiously at each other and tried to communicate, the Tibetan girls combing their long wrinkly hair.

Most evenings were spent with the few other travellers in the kitchen of the rival Tibetan Guest-House. Why we sat in the kitchen when there was a dining-room outside, I do not know, but that is how it was, and I loved the atmosphere there. It was a dark shack lit by one light bulb and by the flaming fire on which dinner was cooked. We helped ourselves to bowls of meat and vegetables which were fried up in a wok (with ladles of soya sauce and monosodium glutamate) by an enormous Tibetan wrapped in a grease-spattered apron. Another man then looked in the bowl and guessed a price, and another waved a kettle of sweet milky tea which resembled Indian chai. We sat on rickety wooden benches in the gloom while water from the drains trickled through the tin roof, down a pole and along channels in the mud floor. The great moment came at about 8 p.m. when the huge cook picked up a hunk of yak meat and laid it on a tree stump in the middle of the room. Then with a long-handled axe he hacked the meat to pieces.

I liked meeting the other foreigners here, pooling experiences and information about Tibet. Several people had also

Sacred symbols decorate typical Tibetan house, dominated by Gyantse's ruined *dzong*.

Monks restoring Buddha statue, Gyantse.

At Gala, en route for Nepal.

Above Gala, looking south towards Sikkim.

Yaks, mainstay of Tibetan economy, dressed up for ploughing.

Yak dung in round patties, drying for fuel on rooftops, Sagya.

Tingri East, one of the thousands of monasteries destroyed by the Chinese.

Thong La, at almost eighteen thousand feet. Prayer flags are offered as thanks for a safe arrival.

come up from Golmud with tales of breakdowns and snow, and a couple had come from Chengdu, a gruelling journey lasting nine days. There were several hippies too; Bulla, for example, was a Californian Vietnam veteran. He was also a reincarnation of a Tibetan lama, a freedom fighter from a Polish ghetto, and Big Chief Sitting Bull. He dressed entirely in Khampa clothes, the *tuba*, the boots, the sword; even his long blond hair was tied in a wool plait and wrapped around his head. He wandered through Lhasa smiling at the world.

There was also Thinlay, a 22-year-old Tibetan monk from the Dalai Lama's own monastery in Dharamsala. His shaved head was completely round and he joked a lot. Apart from his robes it was hard to remember he was a monk. Thinlay was born in India and brought up in Dharamsala, his education paid for by a German sponsor whom he had never met, but to whom he wrote from time to time.

'An American woman also sent me some money,' he told me, 'but then she wrote and asked me to send her details about my life. I wrote back and told her that if she wanted to send me money she must do so freely, and not expect me to have to give her anything in return.'

'What happened?'

'She didn't send any more.'

Aged sixteen he entered the monastery, and by saying extra prayers for people had managed to save enough money to visit his homeland and relatives for the first time.

The Chinese are now issuing Tibetans with year-long visas in the hope they will be tempted to stay, which would improve the Chinese world image.

Thinlay was shocked by what he saw in Tibet; Tibetan culture, he said, was now more alive outside Tibet than in.

'But there's a more liberal regime now so perhaps things will get better,' I suggested hopefully.

'For the moment they have stopped persecuting the people,' he agreed, 'but now they try a more subtle approach: education. All school lessons are conducted in Chinese. Chinese is the official language. I have even met Tibetans who cannot speak Tibetan.'

I remembered the market and the Barkhor and the Jokhang; they had seemed so lively and robustly Tibetan, but I had to admit that many people were wearing khaki Chinese trousers under their coats, and little black cotton shoes, and many others were dressed entirely in Chinese clothes. Perhaps the Chinese and Tibetan parts of town were not so different after all. The shops and markets were flooded with cheap mass-produced Chinese goods, far more practical than the Tibetan coats and hefty boots. I also remembered noticing in the Jokhang a huddle of monks praying before an altar. They were sharing the warmth of two blankets – Chinese blankets. Their tea was in a Chinese thermos, and their shoes, placed neatly beside them, were Chinese shoes. Gradually the Tibet Autonomous Region is being brought into line with the rest of the country. Perhaps the Tibetans will soon become another forgotten minority group absorbed into the Chinese masses, their clothes worn only by song-and-dance troupes for tourists.

The day after meeting Thinlay I was walking through the back streets behind the Jokhang when I noticed a monk trying to attract my attention. He seemed filled with the excitement of a secret and I followed him into a small temple, just one room, to see a new Buddha statue being built. Seated on the altar was the wooden frame, while below some young monks were screen-printing sheaves of prayers that would fill its hollow insides. I asked who pays for this restoration, but they could not understand. A woman's voice interrupted, 'The Tibetan people of course.'

It was as if the sibyl had spoken, I was so surprised to hear English. A middle-aged woman dressed in Chinese trousers and jacket, hiding behind a dust mask, was standing in the doorway. We spoke for a while and she told me she had learnt English in Darjeeling during the 1950s when she had lived there for three years; now she spoke with an Indian accent.

'My husband was working for the Tibetan government, and

I was just a simple housewife. But Lhasa is changing,' she observed. 'This year is the first time I have seen young people like you here.'

'So you haven't had much chance to practise your English then.'

'No. If the Chinese knew I had been to a foreign country I would have been tortured.'

Without another word, she hurried away. I was left dumb-founded. She had looked so respectable in her Chinese clothes that I had carefully avoided any controversial subjects and uttered the usual platitudes, but her few words brought shock-ingly home the horrors of the invasion and the Cultural Revolution that I had read about but could not really believe. In 1959 all surviving males between the ages of sixteen and sixty who did not flee abroad and did not collaborate were im-prisoned, most deported to China. Many died of starvation in Chinese road gangs. Those who remained were subject to Maoist deprogramming and self-accusation sessions. I longed to know more about this woman's experiences – why she had returned to Tibet, what had happened to her and her husband. I had promised to come back the next day with aspirins for another woman in the temple and I hoped the English-speaking woman would be there.

I did not see her when I arrived, but I sat beside a stone well in the little courtyard outside the temple, and waited. After a while she appeared. She did not seem particularly surprised to see me, or particularly pleased, but she chatted as before. We did not mention the Chinese, but discussed the weather, the possibility of more snow. Then she stood up and said she must do her shopping, and left.

I could not resist going back again the next day, but the temple was closed, and no one was there. I waited a few days before returning but when I did, she was there again. This time we sidled up to the subject of Tibet, and I remarked on the noticeably few places to eat in Lhasa. She said that traditionally pilgrims and visitors could rely on cooking for themselves or finding lodgings and food in other people's homes, so there was no need for restaurants. She hesitated a moment.

'Would you like to share a bowl of noodles and experience Tibetan hospitality?'

As she expected, I jumped at her offer. She lived in this same courtyard up a steep flight of wooden steps leading to a rickety balcony.

'This building was the home of one family once,' she explained.

'Now ten or even eleven families live here. We have one room each.'

She opened a low wooden door, and for a moment I could see nothing in the dark interior.

'Please, sit down. Make yourself at home.'

I deciphered a low bench against one wall behind a knee-high wooden table painted shiny red. Gradually I began to make out the rest of the room, its walls painted sea-green, a cupboard decorated with green and red and blue flowers and glossy with varnish. It reminded me of other folk art, Hungarian or Scandinavian. Shelves displayed copper and aluminium pots. The end of the room was hidden behind a curtain, but I could see a bed and, in the furthest back region, a small stove on which she brewed some soup.

She sat beside me, and for a few minutes we drank and said nothing. Then she put down her bowl and sat back and looked at me. She had a broad square face under collar-length permed hair.

'Now we can talk.'

'Surely you aren't still afraid of the consequences?'

'No, at the moment things are better. We have a new Leader appointed this month, a younger man. But you never know when things may change. Three years ago everything seemed better, then suddenly the government rounded up hundreds of so-called criminals and executed them outside Lhasa.'

'But they did that all over China, not just here. I mean, it wasn't a clampdown only on Tibet.'

'No, but a lot of people they shot were not criminals. They were suspected so-called "political activists".'

'So now you don't trust them?'

'Now we have to be careful. We wait and hope. We must live together peacefully, try to forget the past, and hope the Chinese will begin to understand our people. Don't think I am anti all Chinese. As in every group of people there are good and there are bad. Certainly things are better now – people in Lhasa are no longer starving, there is food in the market.'

'Do you think the Dalai Lama will return?'

'No, for the moment, no. But we hope. Our history is long, and we have suffered many things. Thirty years is a short time for us.'

'How can you be so patient?'

She gave a bitter little laugh and did not answer. We sat in silence.

'I'm sorry,' I blurted, 'this seems to be like an interview or an interrogation, but I have so many things to ask, and Tibetans who speak English are so few.'

She smiled.

'What I hope is that you will tell the people of your country what life is like for us here.'

'There is another thing I'd like to ask. Why did you return to Tibet at such a difficult time? Why didn't you stay safely in Darjeeling?'

'We saw what was happening here, and at first we were pleased at the reforms. Like many educated Tibetans we knew reforms were necessary, so we returned to our country to help. Also my husband's job came to an end.'

'But why didn't you escape in 1959? You could have gone back to Darjeeling.'

'You don't understand. Leaving your homeland when it is in trouble is like – what is that expression – a rat leaving a sinking ship. Not that I blame others for going, and of course the Dalai Lama had to leave. They would surely have killed or imprisoned him which would have been no use to anyone.'

'Do you regret staying?'

She did not answer for a while. The pause grew uncomfortable and I regretted this impertinent question. Then she spoke in a cool, manner of fact voice.

'My husband was imprisoned. He was tortured. He was released after fifteen years but was so weak that he did not live for long. He died five years ago.'

'I'm so sorry.' Everything I thought of saying sounded trite.

'He was denounced by a one-time friend, someone who turned collaborator. We did not have any children. Life was hard. But to answer your question, No, I don't think I regret it.'

She stood up, smoothing down her Chinese trousers, and said abruptly. 'And now I think you had better go. I have many things to do. I am sure you have too.'

I tried to thank her, but there was no time. She said goodbye briskly, and shut the door. I had been dismissed. I climbed slowly back down into the courtyard to be absorbed once more into the bustling market. I did not see her again.

Back at the guest house someone handed me a book on which had been scrawled 'Chinese lies'. It was the Chinese version of their achievements in Tibet – exactly what Martin had spouted in Xian. It praised their freeing of Tibet from feudal servitude to the monks, and from imperialist aggression. By this I suppose they meant the British who, since the Younghusband expedition at the beginning of the century had kept two representatives in Lhasa. The book described the subsequent economic growth and prosperity, the building of the airport and now the road and railway line, no mention of course of the heavy taxes extracted from the Tibetans to help pay for all this which, combined with a disastrous agricultural policy, created two decades of famine and starvation.

– 15 –

Drepung and Nechung

Five miles outside Lhasa and, like the Jokhang, in the process of being restored, is Drepung Gompa, one of the three great monasteries of the reformed Gelukpa or 'Yellow Hat' sect which ring the city of Lhasa.

It was once the biggest monastery in the world, a university housing ten thousand monks who came here from all over Tibet to study for their 253 vows and their degrees. Now a few hundred monks remain. The rest fled abroad or were publicly humiliated, forced to renounce their vows, tortured, imprisoned, or killed. Drepung and Sera at least survived; their sister monastery Ganden, 'Place of Joy', the first Gelukpa monastery founded by Tsong Khapa himself, has been completely destroyed. It was blasted by dynamite and pillaged by Chinese and Tibetans alike. It is said that if monks refused to destroy their own monasteries, they were beaten, sometimes to death.

I went to Drepung with the Number Two leader of my guest house who spoke Chinese and a little English so we could just understand each other and communicate with the monks. This man had himself been a novice at Drepung, sent there at the age of eight. It was normal for one of several sons to be educated in a monastery while the others stayed to help on the land. He remained there until the Chinese arrived four years later. Another worker at the guest house had warned that this man was a collaborator, and so I must be careful of what I said about the Chinese. He always referred to the Chinese invasion as 'Liberation'.

Through bruise-coloured snow clouds we drove in his jeep to the monastery which spread out like a large village under the sheltering curve of a mountain. These three monasteries were the first to be built in a valley and not at the top of an isolated crag.*[1] But as the clouds swept past, occasionally thinning for a moment, I glimpsed a building high up on the mountain, a remote outpost, a *tsamkhang*, a retreat for the monks from the worldly valley below. In an unexpected shaft of sunlight, the golden roofs gleamed greenish against the barren brown earth behind. Then the clouds closed in again, and let fall thick, suffocating flakes.

Looming through the snow came boulders painted red and blue in the image of Buddha and a staircase of temples, the perspective of whose leaning walls extended their stern and dwarfing height. Built along the same lines as Tibetan houses, they are inward-looking, turning their backs on the bitter winds, sheltering monks in paved courtyards. Inside are the treasure-houses themselves, dim-lit interiors rich with smells, the walls painted in brilliant colours with Buddhist stories; sacred symbols; the wheel of life; the eighteen hells, each with its own special torture. Deep red pillars were festooned with hangings, *khatas* dangled from the idols, and Buddhas beneath golden canopies crowded on to altars among coins, mandalas, postcards of other temples and photographs of the Dalai Lama, wearing his incongruously modern black-rimmed spectacles, all flickering in the light from silver dishes of yak butter, spread out in rows of seven. As in most great religions seven is a sacred number. There were forty temples in all, and their richness made Kumbum seem bereft. Some were lined with shelves of prayer books. These were each about two feet long, loose-leaf and handwritten, held together between wood blocks and covered with silk or brocade. Other temples were portrait

*1. *Gompa* means Monastery, but is literally translated as 'house in solitude'.

galleries with sinister painted busts of holy lamas, their glassy eyes staring out of waxen faces. Perhaps it is like this in many desert places: the drier and more monochrome the landscape, the more colourful and decorated become people and interiors.

Pilgrims circled the temples measuring out gifts of butter, barley grains, pins and needles and bracelets. A monk assured me that these offerings have no significance in themselves; they are simply what the people have to give. In one temple they circled a sacred shrine, bending low to touch it with their foreheads, and a monk poured into their cupped hands purifying water which they drank or tossed over their heads. The smallest temple of all was also the oldest, a tiny room grafted on to a rock on which was carved an image of Buddha. A monk sat in one corner chanting prayers.

'When was the Buddha carved?' I asked him.

'It was not carved,' he replied. 'It sprang out of the rock on its own.'

In the cavernous assembly hall small cushions were being laid out on parallel rows of ankle-high benches. The room was being prepared for prayers and I was asked to leave. I sat outside and listened to the monks entering from another door, sitting down and talking amongst themselves. A deep bass voice began to chant and the monks joined in; a drum started beating as their prayers resonated through the hall, growing faster and faster to a climax of clashing cymbals, ringing bells, pounding drums. Then silence, and the chanting began again. The excitement and power of those sonorous voices never ceased to intoxicate.

In Nepal, in temples of the unreformed 'Red Hat' sect, I had heard the horns and conch shells blown, and the bass boom of the *Ragdong*, the seven-foot-long horn. I never heard them in Tibet but I read that they are now being blown once more.

When eventually the chanting ended I ventured back into the hall but no one was there. The only sign of the monks was the regular mounds of their yellow cloaks, abandoned where they sat. Perhaps they had chanted themselves away, melted into yellow pats of yak butter like Little Black Sambo's tigers.

Butter plays a regular part in Tibetan life. Not only is it one of the staple foods, and used to make candles, but the colour yellow symbolises purity and growth. The *Cholung*, the Tibetan history books, compare the creation of the earth with the making of butter. Earth was created from an ocean which a strong wind whipped up into a froth-like cream, and then turned the cream into butter. Thus land was formed.

It was the 'pure' Yellow Hat sect which in the fourteenth century established the monastic pattern: celibacy, limiting tantric practices – the use of special secret rites – to only the most self-disciplined and ascetic, and emphasising meditation and study. The community at Ganden grew so fast that Drepung and Sera were built to accommodate all the monks. Monasteries were the centres of teaching, and until the Chinese arrived there was little or no secular education. But these monks were far from unworldly; secular and religious life was inextricably entwined. Until 1959 monks were often occupied with trade, commerce and farming as well as performing rites for the dead and praying for the welfare of the living. The abbots of Drepung, Ganden and Sera, with the Lhasa nobles, also formed the government's inner cabinet, and every New Year Drepung used to take over the government, the monks acting as police – *dobdobs* – and very brutal they are said to have been.

The few monks I met sidled up and murmured 'Dalai Lama picture, Dalai Lama picture'. Unfortunately I had no picture to give. This is what Tibetans most desire, a recent photograph of their spiritual and temporal leader, even though many have never seen him. It is common for people to wear Dalai Lama badges and lockets; until recently only Chairman Mao would have been allowed.

Four young monks lounged against a backdrop of temples and I asked if I could take their picture, whereupon one of them sprang to attention and ruined the relaxed pose. I took it anyway, and then he held out his hand. He thought my camera was a polaroid, and showed me a picture some other nice tourist had taken. He was disappointed.

At that moment another monk with a face like a horse came up and demanded I paid twenty yuan per photograph. That would have cost me about £200, and as I had not been warned earlier, and had given plenty of donations, I refused. Poor Sonam, the collaborator, was forced to translate, and even he confessed in the end that this monk was not a real monk but an official. I had been feeling guilty about being there, looking, spoiling, intruding, but now I began to wonder if the whole monastery was staged for the tourists. I went into the kitchens, but where in Ladakh and Nepal tea would have been brewing, here everything seemed to be derelict. Perhaps the monks went home in the evenings.

Just below Drepung is Nechung, Drepung's protecting deity and once the state oracle. If any state decision was to be made, or an auspicious date for an event chosen, the Dalai Lama and his government would consult Nechung. Even the decision whether or not to leave Tibet in 1950 was taken here. A monk was the medium for the oracle, and he was said to have writhed and frothed as the oracle took hold of him to make its prophecies. Now Nechung is a few scruffy buildings with a cow tethered to a wall under a hovering smell of dung. I wandered into a *tasha*, or living quarter, and found a man cooking his lunch on a primus. He was not a monk but a caretaker. Another building housed only leering boys and a terrifying little watchdog which chased me away.

– 16 –

The Sky Burial

Every morning except Sunday, as the sun rises, one of the most bizarre of Tibetan rituals still takes place: the Sky Burial.

It was still dark when I slipped out of the guest-house and walked through the deserted city towards the Chinese suburbs. As the dark paled to grey, nomads emerged from their yak-hide tents to huddle round early morning fires. Chinese men appeared on the road to practise *Tai qi*. I walked steadily on for over an hour until the last of the tin-roofed commune buildings trailed behind me. I looked to my left across an expanse of wasteland and saw, under the mountains, a wisp of smoke and some silhouetted figures. That was the place. As it came nearer the figures developed features: there were two rough-looking types in ripped trousers and bare feet, and two filthy raga-muffin children, gathered round a fire brewing tea. They did not greet me or smile. Close by was a wide flat rock propped up by a stone column like a dolmen. On it lay a curiously-shaped white bundle.

Slowly the sun came up over the mountains behind us, a shaft of golden light catching the highest point in the valley, the Potala, as it hovered weightless above the still dark and misty city.

A Toyota jeep roared up and out stepped three Chinese cadres, as trendy and rich-looking as Hong Kong Chinese. We greeted each other and I asked where they were from.

'Lhasa,' the girl snapped. Her two friends were visiting from Kunming. We waited, and I ambled away up the side of the hill above the rock. One of the Tibetans started shouting and scrabbling up after me. He gestured that no photographs were allowed, snatched my camera bag, and took it back to the fire where he kept it beside him. I was annoyed. I knew this rule, and had not intended to take a picture. One of the Chinese men explained, 'We are allowed to take photographs, but it is forbidden for foreigners to do so.'

'That's discrimination I think,' I said in my sourest voice. They did not reply.

Normally nobody was allowed to take pictures. A group of photojournalists from Beijing had recently been chased away with burning logs and the windows of their bus were smashed. Clearly these three cadres were different, and one of the Tibetans played up to them, amusing them, telling his life history. He had been a truck driver before taking up this, the most despised of Tibetan professions.

The other man walked around the rocks leaving deposits of *tsampa*, roasted barley flour, and lighting fires of sweet-smelling juniper wood. The boy, who looked like a gypsy child, disappeared behind the rock and returned wearing a man's jacket, several sizes too big. The older man shouted at him and took the jacket, putting it on himself. Then they finished their tea and straggled down to the rock. As the sun hit us at exactly eight o'clock, the man unleashed a knife as long as a sabre and strode up to the white bundle. Already waiting, hunched on the brown hillside, were the vultures, hundreds of them.

He took hold of the bundle, slashed the ropes and unrolled it. Inside was the dead body of a girl. She was fully clothed and trussed up in a sitting position as though meditating. He removed her corduroy Chinese shoes and tried them on. They were too small so he threw them down to the boy who gleefully wore them – though on the wrong feet. The body was stretched out, a rope wrapped around its neck and weighted down with a stone. The girl was then stripped, and systematically skinned. An arm was hacked off and the flesh – red but not bleeding – sliced off the bone and laid out across the boulder. The bone was flung to the other man who pounded it to powder with a rock and mixed it with *tsampa*. A smaller bone was thrown to the boy who did the same. The butcher worked steadily, hacking limb from limb and then fleshing it. Meanwhile one of the Chinese cadres, grinning to his friends, crawled over the rock taking close-up photographs. Fortunately there were no monks or mourners here to witness this insulting intrusion. Even without that, to see your own daughter hacked apart must be a horrifying experience. I turned away, sickened. I tried to think of it as meat, but it was a human being, a dead girl. But perhaps I too was ghoulish for I could not resist looking back.

Half an hour, an hour. I lost track. The sun climbed up into the sky, and the butcher paused for a moment to shout at the little girl who scuttled over with a cup of tea. He drained it and returned to work with grim determination. Soon all that remained was the skinned torso which was disembowelled, the guts threaded over the rock. Then he picked up the head by the hair and brandished it aloft for the photographer, and dashed the brains out. It was over. He stood up and waved his bloody knife; the Chinese applauded. Then he bent and snatched a piece of flesh and, holding it high above his head, he let out a piercing cry and flung it into the air. Down came the vultures, huge and mottled with vicious heads and beaks. Flapping their yard-span wings they descended on the human flesh, tearing it apart, squabbling, teeming on the rock.

Not far away across the valley, within sight of this sacrificial rock and macabre dissection, the ordinary life of Lhasa, the daily round of breakfast and of going to work, was beginning.

Soon after, the Toyota swept away with the butcher smugly ensconced inside. He had been rewarded with a lift. I sat for a while watching the vultures as one by one they ate their fill and flapped off. Beneath the rock, strewn amongst the scrub, were the ragged clothes of countless dead people – those clothes that the butcher and his son had rejected.

However bizarre, there are practical reasons for the sky burial. Wood is scarce and cannot be wasted on burning the dead, and the ground is often too hard to dig graves. There is also the Buddhist desire to help other living creatures even in death. It is considered a bad omen if even the smallest morsel is left uneaten; if anything remains it must be burnt at once. The human spirit is said at this time to be in *Bardo*, a limbo between death and rebirth that lasts for a minimum of forty-nine days – seven times seven. During this time prayers are said daily to try and sustain the faith of the spirit before it enters a new body, but whether or not the soul will reappear in human form depends largely on past deeds which the prayers can do nothing to change. Once the spirit has departed for *Bardo*, the human body itself is of no more interest.

I was mesmerised by those vultures and remained rooted there until the last one had flown off, taking with it the final morsel of flesh for its burial in the sky. Then I too left, making my way over the sandy hillside to Sera Gompa, its gold roofs glistening in the bright morning sun. An old woman sheltered under a willow tree, swinging her prayer wheel, oblivious to all but her prayers. A dog lay asleep beside her, twitching in its dreams. Peace descended after the brutality. Slowly progress-ing through the main temple, I reached the roof-top and looked across the valley again. The Potala was no longer the isolated fairy palace of dawn, but had been absorbed into the humdrum busy city.

In a leafy courtyard below, dozens of young shaven-headed monks laughed and talked and sauntered about. An older monk clapped his hands and they sat down in circles on the ground, one monk standing in the middle. He called out, clapped, stamped his feet, and pointed at someone in his group, who answered back. As Thinlay explained later, they were practising the ancient art of debating and being tested on theological questions.

At the gate a group of women and children sat around stalls selling jellied white noodles covered with chilli sauce. Red and white, flesh and bones: I still felt dazed, unable to shake off images from the morning – the figures around the fire, the sycophantic butcher, the boy in the dead girl's shoes, the knife. At that moment a tour group materialised from nowhere and descended like the vultures on to the Tibetans, brandishing their cameras. As one took a photo so the others rushed over to see what they had missed, clustering round the victim. Then they were sucked back into the coach that had disgorged them, and vanished.

I hitched a ride back to Lhasa in an army jeep, and we passed the nomads again. With a long bloody knife they were skinning a yak. I was not being allowed to forget what I had seen.

– 17 –

Farewell to Lhasa

My days in Lhasa passed swiftly, sight following sight, temple following temple. The snow clouds evaporated, and skies turned crystal blue. I wished Patrick could have been here, he would have loved it so; I made frequent trips to the No. 1 Guest-House in case he had sent a letter but there was nothing. There was also nothing from my family – I had not heard from them for nearly two months. It was on a day such as this, feeling a little sad and lonely, that I celebrated my twenty-fifth birthday. Quarter of a century!

I was determined to forget it, but could not resist returning to the poste restante again. The letter drawer was, they assured me, locked. For some reason I was suddenly determined that drawer should be opened.

'We do not have the key,' the Chinese woman insisted.

'Where is it?'

'The person with the key is not here.'

'Where is she?'

'She'll be here at three o'clock. Come back then.'

After arguing for a while, she agreed to have the key by two o'clock. I returned at 2.30 p.m. to find a different woman.

'I do not have the key. Come back at eight o'clock.'

I went back at five, and as I walked in a third woman handed me an envelope as though she knew my name. It was for me! Inside, neatly folded, was a birthday telegram from my family. It said,

HAPPY BIRTHDAY HOPE YOU RECEIVED LETTER AT BRITISH
EMBASSY PEKING ALL WELL HERE WE LOVE YOU DRYSDALE.

I was so overjoyed I kissed the woman. To receive a telegram in
Lhasa, on the roof of the world, and on the very day of my
birthday – it seemed a miracle.

So I did celebrate after all, drinking beer in the Tibetan
Guest-House with two Australians, Andrew and Sarah, who
shared my dormitory and had become friends. Talk was all of
Tibet, and I began to feel it was time to move on, to leave Lhasa
and see more of the country. This however was very difficult,
largely because of Chinese restrictions. Only Lhasa was
officially open, though some tour groups were taken south-
west to Shigatse.

Thinlay had come via Shigatse and Gyantse from Nepal,
and he warned of frequent police checks along the route. It was
permitted to go there, however, if one was leaving the country
and had an exit visa stamped for Nepal. I calculated that if I
travelled for a week or so, I would still have time to get back to
Beijing for the trans-Siberian. But if I was not leaving for
Nepal, I would not have an exit visa. I pondered this problem
for a while. There was another difficulty too: the lack of public
transport. It was possible to get lifts in trucks going to the
Nepalese border, but these would drive straight through,
allowing no time to see anything along the way. Hitching from
place to place was said to be almost impossible. An Englishman
who tried this had returned to Lhasa after sitting at the
roadside for three days seeing nothing but an occasional mule.
I would have to hurry, and I kept my ears open for a solution.

I was lucky. On going into Snowlands one day I bumped into
a German called Jurgen. He was in a state of excitement
because he had spotted an old bus in a yard and found its
Tibetan owner, who agreed to hire it out for a minimal sum.
If several of us hired it – and we would be bound to fill it
with others who wanted to reach Nepal – we could take as
long as we liked, and go where we wanted, roads and check-

posts permitting. It could not have been a more perfect solution.

'There is one problem: I want to come back to Lhasa, and not leave the country,' I said.

'That's all right because you can come back with the bus.'

'But I can't go to these places unless I am leaving the country. I'll be deported if I'm caught. It doesn't matter if you are caught in a closed place and deported, because you want to go to Nepal anyway.'

'That's easy. You get yourself an exit visa, then say that when you reached the border the friend you were going to meet was not there, so you decided to come back to Lhasa.'

It seemed a good idea. I went to the Public Security Bureau out beyond Lingkhor and with no trouble had my passport stamped with an exit visa. I did not bother to get a Nepalese entry visa as I did not think I would use it.

Jurgen put up a notice in the guest-house and the bus was quickly filled, some people going to Nepal, others just for the ride. Confident though we were, we did have very little information about the route. The typed sheets Martin had given me were useful, and Thinlay, who had passed through many of the places on his way to Lhasa, had decided to come with us. But that was all. My map marked no more than the main towns and the road between them, but Jurgen (or Joggy as he was known) was sure there was a lower road that went down towards Sikkim and Bhutan and then ran along the south just under the Himalayas, and it was this route we would try to take. The only thing we knew was that there would be little food along the way except *tsampa* and yak butter tea, so having learnt my lesson, I stocked up on tins of fruit and dried noodles, filled my water bottle and bought a dust mask.

I had one thing still to see before leaving: the Potala. I crossed the town and climbed the flights of zigzagging steps that slowly and breathlessly brought closer the blinding white walls – thirteen storeys high – until at last they disappeared above me. I faced a pair of massive carved doors propped open and draped with a heavy red and gold cloth, which was looped to one side with a red tasselled rope. Coming in from the blinding light, for a few seconds I could see nothing, but I could smell the musty odour of long disuse. Gradually my eyes cleared, and I saw a windowless passage with a rough unsurfaced floor. This led to the temples.

There were dozens of them, each more gloomy and oppressive than the last. They had, I read, always been so, and the Dalai Lamas disliked being incarcerated in this mausoleum, preferring the sun-lit gardens of the Norbulinka, the Summer Palace. Now that the Potala is no longer the heart of Tibet, it is sadder and gloomier than ever. There was a pervading sense of death. Dust-covered *chortens* were filled with the remains of successive Dalai Lamas; a monk walked past holding a polished cranium. I supposed he was enacting some sinister tantric rite, but Thinlay explained later that the skulls of worthy lamas are often preserved as objects of meditation.

In a tiny shrine was the most holy object here, the eighteen-inch-high statue of Chenresig, the Bodhisattva or *Changchub Sempa* who was sent by Buddha to save the Tibetan people from Bon practices and to set them on the path to enlightenment. The Dalai Lama is said to be the reincarnation of Chenresig, the lord protector of Tibet. The first Dalai Lama or *Gyalwa Rinpoche*, Ocean of Wisdom, was 'discovered' by a fifteenth-century Mongolian king. Reincarnation solved the problem of succession for the celibate Gelukpa sect; the unreformed Red Hat sects could pass the position of abbot down from father to son. Where no son could (or should) exist, reincarnation was the perfect solution.

Even the Dalai Lama's own suite of rooms were deathly, kept as they were when he left, the clock stopped at the hour of departure as though he himself had died and his people were struggling to keep their memory of him alive. But I was being morbid: perhaps the rooms were preserved for his return when he could pick up where he left off, and the time in between would be blotted out. The floors of his sitting-room and bedroom were strewn with *khatas* and pilgrims crowded round the rope barrier to look. For a Bodhisattva and a ruler they were surprisingly small and unpretentious, the rooms of a simple man. Only one noble, coincidentally the son of the Mongolian king, has ever been the chosen one; the present Dalai Lama was born of a poor peasant family found in a farmyard in Amdo, near Koko Nor, after a vision in a sacred lake revealed his whereabouts. It was only days after his inauguration that he was forced to flee.

In one dark sanctuary I thought I was alone, but suddenly came upon a monk crouching in a corner. He was saying his prayers to himself as he made wicks for the butter candles. He smiled, and in a whisper asked if I was American. The monks often asked that. '*Yingi*, English,' I replied, and he nodded with all the knowingness of incomprehension, and gestured me to wait. He turned to a drawer, delved around, and brought out a bowl of sweets.

'*Tukchechay*,' I thanked him, and offered the sweet to the Buddha. No, no, it was for me to eat, so I thanked him again, and in return bought a *khata* which I rolled into a ball and flung at the god, as is the custom. I missed, and he laughed and retrieved it, and we tried again. His eyes gleaming in the darkness, this friendly monk then burrowed around in the drawer again and produced an old Tibetan coin. This too he gave me. These coins have been out of circulation since the Chinese arrived.

But he had not finished. Assuming I would want to take an illegal photograph of the Buddha, he crept over to one door and quietly closed it, then crossed to the other door to stand guard while I took the picture. He greatly enjoyed this subterfuge.

Shaking his hand and saying goodbye, I left the palace, blinking in the sun. Below me was the screeching and hooting of traffic and the glittering tin roofs, wafts of incense and dung and petrol and, further away, every detail now visible in the clear light, the ring of mountains. I sat for a while in the park at the foot of the hill. An old man twirling his prayer wheel talked for a long time to a bird that perched on the branch of a willow tree; an old woman carved *Om mani padme hum* on pieces of slate, and I bought one off her. I felt an inexplicable melancholy, reluctant now to leave Lhasa. Perhaps I subconsciously suspected I would not return: we were off the next day.

– 18 –

Across Tibet to Nepal

It was 6.30 a.m. and still dark when eleven of us – a mixed bag of travellers – gathered at the hotel entrance to wait for the bus. Everyone was excited. I asked the girls who slept in the reception room to look after my pack; if I was coming back to Lhasa there seemed no point in taking it. But just as we were leaving I suddenly decided to take it after all; it would be no trouble in the bus, and it was safer to keep it with me.

The bus was even more derelict than the one from Golmud. The entire back window was missing (the gap patched over with cardboard), the door did not close properly and the sides were pitted with rust holes. We were a tour group with a difference: a wrecked bus and a bunch of dirty, travel-worn people with white dust masks over their noses and mouths, and a strange assortments of hats and scarves on their heads. Several, like me, were trussed up in blue Chinese jackets. An English boy called Paul slumped on the seat in front of me: he had been up late with some Tibetans drinking *chang*, barley wine. Thinlay, to my surprise, had taken off his robes and looked like the rest of us, in jeans and a T-shirt with 'Support the Winter Olympics' decorating his chest. It was hard to remember he was a monk, but he had his visa to prove it. Profession: Monk.

There were two drivers, both with pock-marked faces and eyes hidden behind dark glasses which were never removed, day or night. They had been scarred by a battery that had exploded in their faces and showered them with acid. They were quite without charm. I sat near the back uncomfortably close to a stinking yak skin filled with butter. Its Tibetan owner sat beside it; he was hoping for a good sale somewhere along the route.

Our bags were strapped on to the roof and we set off along the Kyichu river towards Gyantse. A soft pink streak spread across the sky and from time to time the sun itself was visible between the mountains; it lit up the twists and ribbons of mist that hung suspended and almost tangible in the river valley. A giant blue Buddha painted on a cliff-side met its quivering reflection below, crossed by two men in a small yak-skin coracle, square shaped, curving up at the corners and very unsteady.

Slowly the softness turned to harsh clarity, the sky a dense impenetrable blue, and by midday we had crossed the Tsangpo (the Brahmaputra) and were climbing up into the mountains towards the 15,500 foot Kamba La, the first of two passes we must struggle over before reaching the border. Not a touch of green, of grass or trees, was visible as the road wound relentlessly up and round the barren sand-brown mountains. At last the bus could climb no higher, and we had to abandon it in the hope that without our weight it could heave itself up. So we walked, gasping, up to the crest and there below us spread a turquoise lake, the Yamdrok Yumtso. I have never seen such a blue, the unbelievable blue of a tinted photograph. The surface stretched taut, unbroken by a single reed or ripple. Blue and brown, they were the only colours here, the blue of sky and water, and the brown of the mountains sandwiched between. But far away in the distance white glittered on zigzag peaks; the Himalayas.

Marking the pass were dozens of curious mounds of stones, small, neatly-stacked pyramids. They looked like ancient cairns, or the remains of a child's game. There were also bushes of sticks and coloured prayer flags. Thinlay explained the stones were *labtse*, placed here with the sticks and flags as offerings to the *Lha*, the gods who guard and protect all passes and dangerous places. The flags were coloured according to the year in which the donor was born. Each year is named after one of the elements, and each element has its own colour.

For several hours, while waiting for the bus to reappear, we sat on the pass overlooking the hook-shaped Yamdrok and our pale yellow track that scarred the hill as it spiralled down towards it. Joggy meditated among the *labtse*; before coming to China he had studied meditation in Thailand. In real life he lived beside a lake in Bavaria and sold ice-creams in a shop.

Most of us had been travelling alone until now and felt surprised to be thrust into a group so suddenly, but also quite intrigued. We now had to cope with group decisions and with living intensively with other people. Inevitably factions developed, and quickly the different characters emerged: naughty Paul, bossy Ann, jolly Julie, greedy Graham. Some I had met already, others became friends. Graham was a New Zealander who had taught English in Lhasa for a few weeks; there were two English botanists; there were my two Australian friends; there was a distinguished-looking Irish writer called John, and though he was in his late fifties or early sixties, he did not appear to mind the rigours of the bus. With him was a much younger woman (we never did divine their relationship) who was tall and thin with a plummy voice. She was finishing a Ph.D. on a group of Chinese temples.

'I've also written a history of China from neolithic times to the present day,' she added, in passing.

She was the only one of us to have all the latest camping gear and dust-proof clothing.

'Where did you buy your head torch?' Graham asked politely as she donned her miner's lamp, expecting her to say Hong Kong or New York.

'I got it in an excellent camping shop in Kensington High Street, opposite Barkers, do you know the one?' Embarrassed looks all round. She also was the only one to have a detailed map, but she made it quite clear that no one else was allowed to look at it. She and John were very secretive about their plans.

They wanted to leave the bus along the route, but where they were going, they would not say.

Eventually the bus creaked up to join us, and we wound down to the lake and travelled along its shores for a while. Nothing grew here, and no one was fishing. Traditionally no Tibetans were allowed to fish. To take life was a sin, and to kill fish which were considered sacred creatures was especially bad. But that rule must long ago have been discarded. Perhaps there were no fish in the lake; I noticed a white scum along the beaches, but the water was not salty. Perhaps it was a sacred lake. Thinlay thought there had been a monastery here called Sanding which was lived in by the only female reincarnation. Her spiritual powers not only once prevented the lake from drying up, but also turned her into a pig and her monastery into a pigsty to save them from the Mongols who threatened in 1716. Now the monastery has been destroyed and Dorje Pagmo, the 'Diamond' or 'Most Excellent Sow', has renounced her vows and lives in Lhasa.

We paused only once, beside a puckered glacier that tumbled off the mountain almost down to the road. (A Tibetan girl from the bus was noisily sick beside it.) As we rattled on, so yellow dust billowed in. I was sitting by one of the holes and dust pumped through in choking gusts, coating my clothes, my hair, the insides of my nostrils. I wore sun-glasses against the glare and to keep dust out of my contact lenses, but I was having to wipe the insides of the glasses every ten seconds. By nightfall when we reached Gyantse my hair was matted and grey, and my face covered in a fine layer of powder.

Our first sight of Gyantse was the ruined fort, the *dzong*, clinging to a crag above us and silhouetted against the moonlight. We found our way to the guest-house which stood at its foot, an entrancing haven of candlelight and the familiar pillar-box red beams and columns, red, green and blue striped walls, and floors of smooth dried mud. A group of men ignored us and continued to rattle and clack through a game of dominoes. Others were playing Chinese chequers and swilling *chang*, their shouts of triumph and rage getting steadily louder. I was desperate to wash and found a basinful of hot water boiling in a cauldron above a wood stove in a bedroom. A girl sat in one corner breast-feeding her baby. Meanwhile everyone was clamouring for food. Only available were plain rice and boiled potatoes, and tea that was nothing but hot water, milk and sugar.

I found it difficult to sleep at this altitude, and was awake to hear the woman's voice hectoring out of a Tannoy attached to a pole outside the hotel. Even here, in remote Gyantse, we could not escape the Chinese. I lay in all my clothes under cumbrous blankets, and eventually got up and left the dormitory for the crisp early morning air. The streets were still in shadow, the sun hidden behind the *dzong*. Incense rose from the flat roofs and people prepared for the day's work, opening up stalls in the market. After only one day with the group, I savoured being alone again.

The monastery occupied a hill opposite the *dzong*, enclosed by a fortified wall that looped round the hillside. Inside were only two temples and a ruin, the rest empty rocky space which had once been filled with temples and halls and living quarters. The Chinese had destroyed almost everything. All that remained was a towering Nepalese-style granite stupa, stepped like a wedding cake up to a sheltering golden canopy, and a needle pointing to the heavens. Those sultry Nepalese eyes, Buddha's eyes, watched over the valley. Each layer of the stupa was hollowed out with shrines, and I followed two early morning pilgrims as they circled it, twisting up the spiral staircase layer by layer, to be transfixed by a pot-bellied demon with four shiny red arms and a gold crown balanced above his third eye. I guessed it was Chenresig, for the rudimentary marks of an extra pair of arms are one of the telling signs of a Dalai Lama.

The other temple had not yet opened for the day, so I set off up the hill over the stony rubble to the ruin. A woman waved at me from below, trying to stop me, but I pretended not to see. I pushed open a door and found a straw-strewn passage: animals had been kept here. It led to a large assembly hall. The door was locked but through the cracks I could see the remains of wall paintings, chipped and flaking. Some had been deliberately scratched with a sharp point. I could just make out some Maoist graffiti. A family appeared to live here amongst this ruined glory; I did not see them but heard voices and saw a door hung with carefully tended fuchsias and geraniums. I sat outside for a long time looking down on the town as it came to life, the air resounding with the ceaseless rhythmic cry of a builder as he encouraged his women workers. Gyantse, like Lhasa, was being rebuilt. Though still in its early stages, it looked as if a grand approach to the *gompa* was being constructed – ironic considering the Chinese have destroyed most of what there was to see.

This *gompa* had already been plundered at the turn of the century when in response to Tibetan overtures to Russia, the British invaded. The Tibetans believed magic would keep Younghusband and his expedition at bay, and their mistake cost them hundreds of lives. The British withdrew soon after, leaving two commissioners in Lhasa, and the *gompa* was rebuilt.

Above me, towering against the indigo sky, was a fortification freshly painted red and orange, fluttering with prayer flags. I began to climb up to it. The ground was crumbly shale and disintegrated under my feet. I looked down and saw the now tiny stupa dotted with rotating pilgrims. The hill was so steep and unsafe I was now on my hands and knees, and I was quickly out of breath, my heart pounding. At last I reached the top and collapsed, and my nose began to bleed again. The sky was so limpid that the sun seemed raw and exposed, unprotected by haze or even by atmosphere, and though I had not climbed far, I felt as though I would never again be closer to it. How is it that without sea being anywhere near, one can sense one's height above it?

Precariously balanced on the rocks, I discovered the fortification was just a façade, but up here I could now see the extraordinary formation of the landscape. Like the Lhasa valley it was a long flat plain surrounded by mountains and out of this flatness rose unexpected conical hills. It was on hills such as these that the *dzong* and the *gompa* were built.

The main temple was now open. Some young monks worked under the bright sun on a roof-top courtyard cleaning a Buddha statue. They took it apart, turned it upside down and scrubbed it – so undignified. Dismembering a body: once again the sky burial flashed up into my memory. While talking to the monks, I looked up and saw the sun was ringed by a halo, rainbow-coloured. A rainbow round the sun: surely it was a holy sign. I handed a monk my sun-glasses to see it through but he was not in the least impressed, much more taken by the mirror lenses.

Girls laboured in the market making adobe bricks, or bending down for a man to heap stone blocks on to their backs. Despite the hard work, they were all very cheery. Girls in Tibet laugh a lot, often in a mocking way; they are much more light-hearted than Chinese women. Many wear Chinese Mao caps perched at rakish angles on their heads. In the rest of China these caps are almost sacred, the badge of the good worker and the soldier, and never did I see a woman wearing one. Here women wear them as a joke, as a tourist might. As in many Asian countries, women do as much manual labour as men, though men are usually in charge. According to the Tibetan 'Genesis', woman was originally a man who found his genitals were troubling him so he ripped them from his body and thus became a woman.

Also on sale were longer browner bricks, about nine inches long. I picked one up: it was tea, a brick of tea. There were blocks of grey soap too, and Tibetan clothes, but little else. I had read that Gyantse is a famous wool-producing and textile-manufacturing town. I saw nothing of it, just a woman standing in her doorway, spinning. The old houses were topped by sparse bushes of prayer flags, banned until recently and still paltry compared with the forests of flags waving in the wind over houses in northern Nepal. Under the eaves of several houses were black and white symbols: the lucky swastika, a pyramid of seven balls, a bowl with a circle in it. Tiny rivulets ran between the houses, irrigation channels lined with bright green willow trees. I crossed them, working my way over to the *dzong* and up the steep path to its gates, but they were locked. I particularly wanted to get inside as this was where Alexandra David-Neel had stayed when it was a British garrison, sixty years before. Disguised as a Tibetan, she amazed the authorities by announcing, in English, that she had just spent eight months roaming illegally round the country. I turned away disappointed and spotted an old woman: I pointed inquiringly and she nodded and brought out from the folds of her coat a large key. We toiled back up the hill and she heaved open the doors and disappeared.

If I expected to step into a magic castle, I was soon sickened by what I saw. Buddhas were riddled with bullet holes and walls smeared with graffiti. I left quickly. Down in the valley I heard the hectoring voice again booming down from the *dzong*. Perhaps there had been someone up there with a megaphone. Then I realised it was the speaker outside the hotel, the voice echoing off the hillside.

All the time I was pursued by strings of children demanding Dalai Lama pictures and 'One pen, one pen'. They grabbed my clothes and tugged at my sleeves, laughing and yelling 'Bye bye, bye bye'. They did not know 'Hello'; evidently their teachers had been trying to escape as I now was. They were filthy with matted lousy hair and skin flaking and burnt in the harsh dry air. I found refuge in a tiny restaurant off the market, the walls lined with knee-high benches and tables. An old woman poured out glasses of tea and lifted the lid off a tall stack of metal pots, out of which she brought steamed pasta balls – *momos*. An old man was doing his best to scrape off a bone some shreds of meat which went into the *momos* along with chopped onions. They were wet and filling.

We left at 5 a.m. the next morning, heading south towards Yadong on the Sikkim-Bhutan border. This was the route taken by the Dalai Lama when he fled from the Chinese for the first time in 1950 with a procession of forty nobles, two hundred soldiers, hundreds of servants and fifteen hundred pack animals. It must have been a colourful sight winding through this landscape of muted browns and ochres and yellows; people had laid white stones along his route to keep away evil spirits.

At Yadong we intended to turn west and travel along beneath the Himalayas (assuming there was a road) but we had not driven far before we were stopped at our first army checkpost. It was a Chinese garrison stationed in the middle of nowhere, and one of several we were to come across along the way. Much of the hardship for Tibetans over the last twenty years has been caused by the massive taxes extorted to maintain the several hundred thousand occupying troops. The soldiers looked young, about fifteen years old, but even so we felt nervous. We had now deviated – illegally – off the road to Nepal. They collected our passports; only one person did not have an exit visa, so we slipped his passport in between the others, and nothing was said. We were allowed to continue.

About four hours later we reached Gala, another small village with an army base. We stopped here for two or three hours, climbing out of the bus to be greeted by a welcoming party of old women who stood in line holding their palms together and bowing to each of us in turn saying '*Tashi Delek, Tashi Delek*'. We bowed in reply. Shy smiling children with deep red cheeks clutched each other and hid behind their grandmothers' skirts. But for them, and a terrifying black mastiff that almost choked itself on its chain in desperation to come and savage us, the village was deserted. This was the planting season, and the men and younger women were out in the fields. Accompanied by a troupe of small boys in Chinese hats we climbed the hillside backing on to the village and saw below us pairs of black hairy yaks being driven across the stony ground. The men gripped with bare feet to the thin wooden board behind, and they whistled and trilled as they went, the yaks hurtling along, the red pennants on their necks flying, the scarlet yak-tails decorating their foreheads bouncing. It must say a lot about a people that they dress up their beasts of burden in this way. Decoration of yaks was also forbidden until recently.

The yak is an indispensable beast, able to survive at high altitudes and provide not only labour, wool, meat, butter, yoghurt, and its hide, but also dung. This dries in round patties on the roof-tops like piles of golden coins, or flattened against south-facing walls. In a land where there are very few trees, dung is an indispensable source of fuel, though this leaves nothing to fertilise the fields.

Girls in thick red boots and green scarves were raking the ground to prepare it for the barley. This is Tibet's main crop, producing *tsampa*, Tibet's staple diet. Thinlay had a draw-string yak hide bag filled with *tsampa* which we ate mixed with yak butter and water or with milk and sugar (like semolina). It was nearly as bad as yak butter tea. During the Cultural Revolution it was ordered that barley should be replaced by wheat, a crop unsuited to this thin mountain soil. The little that grew went to fill the state quotas, and famine was the result. Now, as in the rest of China, the land has been returned to the people for them to grow what they choose, and to keep more of it for themselves.

We returned to the bus, but it had disappeared. Someone said dismally that they had seen it going back the way we had come. Surely the drivers could not have left us behind? We still owed them half the money. Joggy went off in search, and returned an hour later having found them back at the army checkpost. They had announced that they refused to go any further on this road, and were taking the upper route, via Shigatse and Tingri to the Nepal border. We were disappointed as now we would see Everest only from a distance instead of right underneath it. We protested, but the more we

argued, the more stubborn and recalcitrant the drivers became. They squatted on the ground and refused to get back
into the bus, so in the end we had to agree, and return to the
Gyantse-Shigatse road. They must have lost their nerve in the
checkpost.

Joggy had also found Maud-Ann, an American, sobbing in
the bus. She was a sad fey woman who was desperately upset
because by coming down to Gala she had missed the Sunday
market in Gyantse. It had been a classic case of majority rule,
and she decided to relinquish her place on the bus to stay until
next week's market. As she had almost no money, we were
concerned about deserting her so far from Lhasa, and weeks
later I met someone who had travelled through Gyantse and
reported sighting a strange American woman. It was poor
Maud-Ann, still there, unable to get a lift out.

Shigatse, the second biggest town in Tibet and capital of
Tsang province, was an ugly dusty Chinese city. Since the
destruction of the fort, which photographs show to have been a
miniature Potala, the only attraction is Tashilunpo, the second
Gelukpa monastery and one of the greatest in Tibet. It is the
seat of the Panchen Lama, generally considered Tibet's 'No.
2', the second spiritual leader after the Dalai Lama. The
Chinese, however, claim him as the leader. Ever since the first
Panchen Lama was found in China in the seventeenth century,
the Chinese have sought to make him their puppet, stirring up
rivalry between the two Lamas. The present Panchen Lama
has spent his life in a velvet prison in Beijing, and when he was
brought to Tashilunpo in 1982 he was expected to make a
dutiful pro-Chinese speech. Instead he bravely reaffirmed the
Dalai Lama's rightful spiritual and political leadership of
Tibet. He was quickly sent back to Beijing, where he remains,
under house arrest.

These ties with China did save Tashilunpo from serious
vandalism, and the multitude of temples remain, a sad reminder of how much has been destroyed at Gyantse. As a
result, Tashilunpo is a showcase monastery. Monks were

chanting in almost every temple, some offering barley grains to the gods, others dedicating round *tsampa*-butter balls over which they sprinkled holy water and said prayers. Another sat beating a drum before a terrifying black giant who wore a necklace of skulls. This was Chenresig in the form of Gonpo, the fierce destroyer of evil. A crowd of monks emerged from a hall dressed in yellow cloaks and a variety of hats, some curving over their faces like extended centurions' hats, others wide and flat like mortar boards. All the monks were old: they were the 200, out of 4,000 monks, who were not deported to China in 1962 for their steadfastly pro-Tibetan politics. They were a dour lot, but they were delighted by the sight of Paul who wore a Khampa's *tuba*.

'*Tuba*! Khampa!' the monks laughed, and hastened to straighten it for him. They were also interested in Thinlay, and questioned him about his monastery and what stage he had reached in his studies.

Thinlay was a *Getsul*, a junior monk. On an average day in Dharamsala he got up long before dawn at about 4.30 a.m. to run for forty minutes to a swimming pool. Then he returned to the monastery for a session of chanting and learning prayers. Then he had breakfast of *tsampa* and tea. Then an English lesson, more prayer-learning, and a test on what he had learnt that day. Then lunch – more *tsampa* and some meat – and then more memorising. Then there was an hour of debating, and yet more memorising. Throughout the day, he had hardly a moment to himself in which to think, or doubt.

I wondered how the Dalai Lama, his own abbot, would view the free way in which Thinlay was travelling with us, wearing Western clothes, sharing mixed dormitories.

'I think His Holiness would not mind as I am learning about the ways of Western people, and I am helping you to understand Tibetan people and Buddhism. But I want to know more,' he said urgently. 'I want to tell you everything I know. But even though I am travelling with Western people, I am determined to keep my vows.'

Lifelong celibacy! What an extreme commitment, especially for someone as seemingly liberated and 'male' as Thinlay.

The *Tsawa Shi*, the four main vows, also include no killing, no lying, and no stealing. He was right to be worried about the corrupting influence of Westerners. As we were leaving Shigatse, the Tibetan woman who ran the guest house boarded the bus and demanded to know the whereabouts of two missing towels. A shamefaced girl reached into her bag and drew one out, and her friend blithely produced the other. Thinlay was deeply shocked. 'That very very bad in Tibet,' he muttered. The rest of us cringed, ashamed at the association of Western people with petty thieving. As for the guilty couple, they had been travelling for so long, and with so little money, that they had lost touch with normal small values. No wonder countries like Bhutan close their doors to foreigners.

Sagya was our next stop, said to be one of the loveliest of *gompas* and villages, seventy miles west of Shigatse along a trail of destruction. The ruined monasteries are recognisable from afar by the groves of green willow trees that have survived amid the wreckage.

It was 10.30 at night by the time we drove into a farmyard. The night was bright and starry, and the river and the mountains and the sleeping village glittered blue-grey. Dazed and tired we climbed out of the bus and up a notched tree-trunk ladder into a candle-lit dormitory and friendly welcome. Tibetan girls dribbled wax down the walls to stick candles against them. Outside the dogs howled.

All Tibetan latrines were holes in the floor above an insalubrious pit. There were no partitions between – they were sociable loos if one could bear to stay and chat, but at least males and females were usually segregated. In Sagya they were not. There were simply a few holes in the ground in one corner of the yard. Later, in Nyalam, one of the English botanists missed her footing in the dark and slid down into a similar hole. It was a most noxious mistake.

That aside, Sagya was an exquisite place. Dozens of tiny

trickling streams fed a clear cold river where yaks were drinking and being washed before heading for the fields. But
destruction of the 900-year-old monastery had been
wholesale; piles of rubble were now loaded on to the backs of
village women to be built into their own walls. But amongst the
debris were deposited heaps of tiny new Buddhas, clay votive
offerings, like seedlings sprouting again after a forest fire. This
is still holy ground. Only one small temple was left, guarded by
a sad old monk and a baby. A boy herded his goats among the
ruins.

On the other side of the river part of the *gompa* had been
reconstructed, and filled with a line of enormous shiny gold
Buddhas. The Sagya sect are not reformed like the Gelukpa,
so are not celibate and the post of abbot is (or was) passed down
from father to son. (Wives and families were kept at separate
establishments, never at the monastery itself.) Being one of the
oldest, it was also one of the most venerated monasteries, with a
famous library of Tibetan and Sanskrit manuscripts, and was
the first to wield political power over Tibet, establishing the
unity of political and religious rule which continued until 1959.

Judging from the state of our bus, we would never make it to
the next village, let alone to the border. We did not mind – most
of us wanted to take it slowly – but the driver had decided he
was in a hurry because some pilgrims were waiting for him at
the border. This was the first we had heard of it, and few of us
believed him. But disputes proved pointless. In the end it took
us five and a half hours to cover 15 miles. The bus broke down
no less than seven times. The driver would lift the engine
cover, peer inside, rev the engine, and then fiddle underneath.
All we could do was hold a torch for him. We sat by the
roadside watching the mule carts steadily overtaking us, and
chatted to farmers and children who appeared apparently from
nowhere to see what was going on and to share our tins of fruit.

For centuries this road has been one of the major trade
routes through Tibet. Caravans of salt and wool passed
through to Nepal in exchange for Nepalese rice. It was this

way, twelve hundred years ago, that Lopon Rinpoche, the great Indian master of Tantrism, had come, subduing the demons that crossed his path. Known in India as Padmasambhava, Lopon Rinpoche was said to have been born in a lotus flower, a fully developed eight-year-old child. His magic powers developed so highly that he alone was considered able to free Tibet from the veil of evil spirits that had frightened away the earlier Indian Buddhist teachers. Lopon Rinpoche was invited to Tibet, and managed to convert the powers of these deities to the good of man, and so allow Buddhism to spread and monasteries to be founded.

I would be ruminating on these demons, wondering if it was they who had jinxed our bus, when the bus came to life. We said goodbye, gathered our belongings, hiccuped along the road a few yards, and then stopped. Then our lights failed as we freewheeled down a ravine in the dark. Someone stood at the front shining a feeble torch through the windscreen, and we screeched to a stop just as we grazed the back of a truck which was parked across the road being loaded with rocks.

Eventually we limped into an army barracks in Lhaze where we collapsed on filthy beds behind a wooden door like the entrance to a garden shed, and laughed and laughed, though none of us knew why. Some small boys heard of our arrival and joined us in the canteen, gazing at our bowls of rice. They were not actively begging or wheedling, just waiting expectantly. We passed them our bowls and they took off their Mao caps and tipped in the rice. One boy then put his cap back on.

Overnight the driver managed to repair the bus and sent his assistant to apologise for yesterday; he himself rarely spoke and had been looking more surly by the day. From then on our journey was fraught with disputes.

We left Lhaze at 5 a.m., dropping off the Irish couple John and Annabel along the way. It was still dark, three hours before dawn, and they heaved out all their luggage to sit on the verge and wait for a lift to wherever they were going. They looked rather forlorn. How long they sat there, far from a village and without any food, I never heard. As the sun stirred behind us, we stopped to brew up salty tea with some farmers, sitting hunched round a fire in a tiny stone byre, the water at this altitude never really boiling.

By midday we reached Tingri East, another perfect village dominated by spectacular ruins. Everest was drawing closer! Tingri is used as a base for Everest expeditions, for last minute supplies and hiring porters, and from here we were to turn south to Rongbuk, the base camp itself. But once again the driver had other plans. Having agreed – and been paid – to go there, he now refused, producing all sorts of excuses: no petrol, he did not know the way, he had to meet the pilgrims. We argued (and crowds collected round the bus to watch, dumbly) but it was no use. Thinlay said the driver was probably afraid of the Chinese authorities. So we continued to Nyalam, intending to reach the Nepalese border by the following morning. Our route now was across a wide brown plateau, and as we passed the small village of Tingri West, so Mount Everest rose in the distance. Nothing but the flat plain came between us and the tallest mountain in the world: Chomolungma, as the Tibetans call it – 29,028 feet. It was a lumpish mass, noticeably higher than the rest of the chain. Steadily the foothills grew until they towered over us and then closed in, blocking the white peaks from view. Blindly we struggled up through these brown mountains and out on to a sandy dome, and there the peaks reappeared alongside us, almost at our elbows – white and solid and hung with heavy clouds. In front of us was nothing but a wall of blue, the only horizon the crest of our track a few yards ahead. But it was always a false crest which, as the dome curved on, never seemed to come any closer. Then at last, by late afternoon, six days after leaving Lhasa, we reached the top. Thong La, at almost 18,000 feet, is one of the highest passes in the world crossable by road. Prayer flags battered noisily to and fro in the bitter wind, and spread before us a sea of golden brown hummocky ridges rolled away towards distant jagged blue-white breakers.

Then it was down again, down into a plunging gorge as the sun set, down towards Nyalam and then towards Nepal, to forests and fields and birds, things I had not seen for months, not since Hainan Island. A spring became a stream and then a racing river. Sand gave way to scrub and then to pine trees and grassy banks on which dew still lay. Silken butterflies twitched about, and red and white Nepalese houses perched above the river and the stepped fields. Colour! Fertility! I suddenly realised how much I had missed them in the parched deserts and cities I had been in for so many months, and could not resist returning to the lush beauty of Nepal.

At Khasa, the small border market, fruit was on sale. Fresh fruit! That too I had not tasted since Hainan Island. Thinlay and I shared a watermelon, but our delight was tinged with sadness for he and several others were returning to Lhasa. Having made up my mind to go on, I did not envy those who stayed. There was no sign of the famous pilgrims, but even though the bus would be empty, the driver had refused to take anyone back. No one knew how long they would have to wait, but some Nepalese, we heard, had been waiting for a lift for nine days. Even if I had wanted to get back to Beijing, it would never have been in time for my booking on the trans-Siberian.

Trading at the border were Chinese in utility khaki trousers, Tibetans in long red coats and hefty boots, and bare-footed Nepalese in jodhpurs and multicoloured hats. The women wore purple, red and blue *lunghis* with bunched sashes round their waists and their hair tied in one long thick plait. *Ni Hao* and *Tashi Delek* were answered with *Namaste*: three languages for three races, each with their own customs, ways of living and of seeing the world. Though the trees and the butterflies ignored this frontier, there can be few where three more different cultures converge.

PLA and police were there in force, and a red flag fluttered over a new and very Chinese customs house. The customs officer checked thoroughly our bags and documents, and then asked if he could practise his English: this was a Chinese outpost, and a sharp reminder that Tibet is now a mere province of the third largest country in the world. I remembered how daunting China had seemed when I was last in Nepal, and how far actually going there had been from my mind.

We all exchanged addresses and promised to stay in touch, and calling out the Tibetan farewell, *Kale pheb*, go slowly, four of us set off on foot across the seven-mile stretch of no man's land, over the Chinese 'Friendship' bridge and along the Chinese-built road that reached to Kathmandu. Though my pack was excessively heavy, weighed down by my padded jacket which was now too hot to wear, I enjoyed walking again after a week of sitting in the bus. Coming off the Tibet plateau and down into Nepal also brought a rush of memories, of trekking with Patrick through landscapes like this, and with it a growing desire to see him again. I missed him and wondered how he was.

A group of bamboo huts rounded the corner, and standing in the middle of the road, legs apart, hands on hips, was the Nepalese Immigration officer. Though his uniform was smart, one of the huts was both his office and his home. We sat on his pallet bed while he stamped the passports and two grubby children ran in and out. He was confused by my lack of a Nepalese visa. I explained that I had changed my plans at the last minute, and suggested he gave me one.

'I have no authority to give you a visa,' he insisted, shaking his head. 'My boss is not here, he has gone anyplace.' He nodded vaguely towards the mountains. 'But don't you have a pen like this one?' He held up a pentel pen. 'Some Japanese friends gave me this. Do you have one for me?'

'I'm sorry,' I said, 'I don't have anything like that.'

'But you must have one. You come from a rich country.'

'But I have been away from my country for a while. All I have is this Chinese biro.'

He looked so downcast that I gave him a sweet and he seemed happy with that, and duly stamped my passport. Then he waved us on, wishing us an enjoyable stay in Nepal: only a few miles from China yet it could be another continent. There was even a four-hour time change.

– 19 –

Kathmandu

Three miles into Nepal we reached the village of Tatopani. *Tato* means hot, *pani* means water . . . a hot spring. There it was, gushing and steaming down towards the river. In no time I was standing under it, washing for the first time in seven dusty days. There was something particularly wonderful about taking a hot shower out in the open in the warm evening air, surrounded by some of the most beautiful landscape in the world. The mountains stretched overhead, ridged with fields, and far up above some tiny white houses caught the last rays of the sun. I was joined by a man with a moustache and a pot belly who sat for hours with the hot water splashing round him, enjoying it as much as I was.

Some of us spent the night in a lodge and hitched a lift to Kathmandu the next morning with an exiled Tibetan called Babu who imported wool. He ran a business in Kathmandu making jumpers which he sold to tourists, and he had hired a new German lorry for the day. On the way we picked up another Tibetan, this one wearing tinted glasses and a large gold ring. He had a brother who lived in California. It was hard to believe they were Tibetan, so different were they from the rough yet proud people stalking the streets of Lhasa.

We paused in Barabishe and looked in at the open-fronted shops that I had forgotten but now remembered. It was a succession of rediscoveries: the women with their bare brown bellies hanging over their saris, the rolls of gaudy fabrics, the bangles and Indian incense, the seething babies, the schoolgirls in prim English uniforms, the Hindi film music trilling from the radios. Everything seemed relaxed yet full of life: I had not one moment's regret for the trans-Siberian.

We reached Kathmandu by late afternoon and I took a room in Thamel and spent the next two weeks doing little more than lying lazily in the sun, more weary after the journey – after all the journeys – than I had realised. I basked in the holiday camp atmosphere in which no one said '*Meiyou*' or made me fill in forms; I was thankful to escape all that. I revisited a few old haunts too; I had forgotten the multitude of sights here. In China one travels for two days to see just one monastery.

But I had also forgotten the number of limbless, leprous beggars, wheeling themselves around on trolleys, tapping on the windows of restaurants. All through China I had seen almost no cripples. Was this grotesque and hopeless poverty the price of freedom of from state oppression, freedom from suppression of religion? I remembered Martin's neat equation: China, Nepal, India, and most third world countries suffer from the same basic problems, too many people from different ethnic groups with not enough fertile land to feed them, yet China is on the brink of becoming a world power. If the other countries followed China's example and wiped out religion, the main obstacle to improving their lot would disappear. No religion equals no poverty. It was simplistic, but faced with squalor that was blamed not so much on a corrupt government and rigid caste system as on a previous life, on karma, and as such to be tolerated rather than changed, I saw his point.

Yet what about the people who now filled the few remaining temples in Gaungzhou and Dongsangfar, the mosque in Xian, the gompas in Tibet? Perhaps people do need something more than Five Year Plans and one-child campaigns to sustain them and give richness to their lives. I noticed more than before the extent of the Tibetan presence in Kathmandu, the thousands of victims of China's totalitarian attempts to 'improve' the lot of the masses and I was left as full of doubts as ever about which was the better system. In several restaurants 'Free Tibet' was plastered on the walls – an empty dream. When one sad-eyed owner heard I had come from Tibet, he grasped my hand and murmured 'Potala, Potala . . .'. Another Tibetan who owned a craft shop refused to bargain until he discovered I had been in Tibet, whereupon the price immediately dropped. He was a Khampa who had fought the Chinese in 1959, and he proudly displayed the bullet wound in his neck.

There was only one thing I wanted to do in Kathmandu, something I had meant to do in Thailand and in Hong Kong. It had nothing to do with China, Tibet, Nepal or India, but with travelling; it was a mission of thanks that I had survived without one bad thing happening to me, almost a penance: it was to visit the Western people in gaol. I did not know who, or how many, would be here, but I assumed someone would have been incarcerated. The prison was on the outskirts of town, distinguishable from the street only by a squad of guards with bamboo shields who stood outside a white neo-classical gateway. They looked curiously at me as I edged past – guiltily for some reason – into a courtyard. Gardens had gone to seed, and guards lay snoozing in dried up flower beds; stucco crumbled off the walls. I asked for the foreigners and was shown to a stone porch. A low chain hung across it. At the other end, about fifteen feet away, was a barred gate. Beyond the gate I could make out a dark stone passage where people and shadows flitted back and forth. Between the chain and the gate sat a few guards, chatting and smoking.

'Who do you want to see?'

'Anyone, it doesn't matter.'

A message was passed on, and Nepalese prisoners, in their own clothes, turned to glance, hoping the visit was for them. A European man paused. 'Hey! Come and say hello.' He looked behind him, wondering who I could be calling to. 'Me?' He was bemused. 'How did you know about us?'

'I guessed there might be somebody here. How many of you are there?'

'We are ten – eight men and two women, all here for the same reason.'

That reason was smuggling gold from Hong Kong to Kathmandu. It was a regular way for destitute travellers to make some money and deals were usually fixed up in Chungking Mansions. While there, I had seen a handwritten notice warning of a gold detector at Kathmandu airport. Someone had scrawled underneath, 'Don't worry, the batteries are flat.' Obviously not flat enough.

The man – his name was John – looked drawn and cowed. He was from the north of England, in his late twenties, and had been here for nine months, though he had still not been tried. There was no doubt he was guilty: the police had picked him up at the airport with two kilos of gold in his shoes. He had no family, and his only visitors were from a Christian mission. The British Embassy sent an official once every three or four months but there was nothing they could, or wanted to, do. He said he had developed a kidney stone from the bad food and water, but had to wait for the Embassy to give permission for an operation. He had now been waiting three months.

If the prisoners had money they could send guards to buy them food and cigarettes, but none of them did have money, which was why they had smuggled in the first place. Things had tightened up recently since three Nepalese had escaped, but prisoners were not treated too badly. Boredom, he said, was the main problem.

The women were kept in a separate area, and the two of them were brought to see me. One was Swiss, an ordinary nice-looking blonde girl such as one saw strolling down the streets of Kathmandu every day. Her stay in Nepal had been extended by two years. Two years! I tried hard to remember back that far, the time that she had spent lying on her bed in the dormitory, sleeping, waiting. She was on the verge of tears as we spoke. She too had had terrible stomach problems, and two operations. She was due to be released that month, and she needed to return to her small village in time for her brother's wedding, or else the neighbours would begin to ask questions and shame her family. Twice her date of release had been postponed.

After nearly two years as the only western woman there, she had been joined three months ago by a Chinese girl from Hong Kong. This girl had met a French traveller, and together they had smuggled gold, something she would probably never have attempted alone. They had secreted the gold internally, but they were detected at the airport. Though they were beaten by the police, something made them hope they could get away with it, and they kept it inside their bodies for eighteen hours. Now they saw each other for ten minutes a day, but they planned to get married in gaol. She invited me to the wedding, but I – free – was leaving Kathmandu. I could hardly bear to tell her so. They were taken away, and I thought with a sickening lurch of relief how easily it could have been me.

My pilgrimage over, I wanted to leave Nepal as quickly as possible, but where was I to go? Returning to Nepal had been a little like returning home: I had spent two months here before, and made friends I was glad to see again. But I slowly realised that I was saturated and could see nothing more; I did not want to overlay China and Tibet with other experiences; I wanted to return to England. I knew I would be back here soon, but now I longed to lie in thick wet grass and to feel the ground spring a bit beneath my feet; I was tired of dryness, and even the colour of Nepal in monsoon time was not enough.

More than that, day by day my thoughts were filled with images and memories of Patrick as I visited the hotel where we had stayed, met friends who had known him, ate in restaurants we had discovered together. I remembered cycling madly through the narrow lanes with our arms round each other, both in Nepalese hats, his staying fixed on his head, mine forever flying off under the feet of wandering cows.

It all seemed years ago. My urge to see him grew and grew,

but I had still heard nothing from him so did not know if he would want to see me. What would he think if I arrived, uninvited, in his country? Perhaps he was even married by now. But why should I worry? I was free to do as I chose. I remembered my thoughts about self-contained actions that need have no purpose beyond themselves. If I want to go and see Patrick, then I must see him; the consequences do not matter. But though I felt I should be behaving so single-mindedly, I also felt that my fate was in some way already decided and that my actions were out of my hands. I needed an oracle, a sacred lake, a medium, to steer me in the right direction. All I had was my own interpretation of events. Like the Wanning villagers in Dongsangfar shaking out a fortune stick and reading their fate, I asked a travel agent to find me a cheap plane to anywhere in Europe. She found me a ticket to Frankfurt, and the train from Frankfurt to London passed through . . . Belgium.

There was nothing for it: leaping in had worked in China, so why not now? But impulsively to decide to leave Asia and cross continents to turn up unexpectedly in Belgium, that seemed almost the biggest leap of all. I left Kathmandu for Delhi, and within twenty-four hours was flying over the almost too green and abundant fields of West Germany and walking dazed through the too plush airport. After nearly a year I was back in the world of money and glamour and sophistication and comfort, and I was overwhelmed. Amazed at my boldness, I picked up a phone (a phone!) and dialled his number. My hands, I noticed, were trembling. What if I had misinterpreted my fate? What if he was not there? What if he was busy? What if he did not want to speak to me? I was drowning in doubt. Then I heard his voice.

'Allo?'

'Hello, it's me!'

'Who is this?'

'It's *me*.'

'What? It's you! Where are you? I have been dreaming about you! I am waiting for you . . .'.

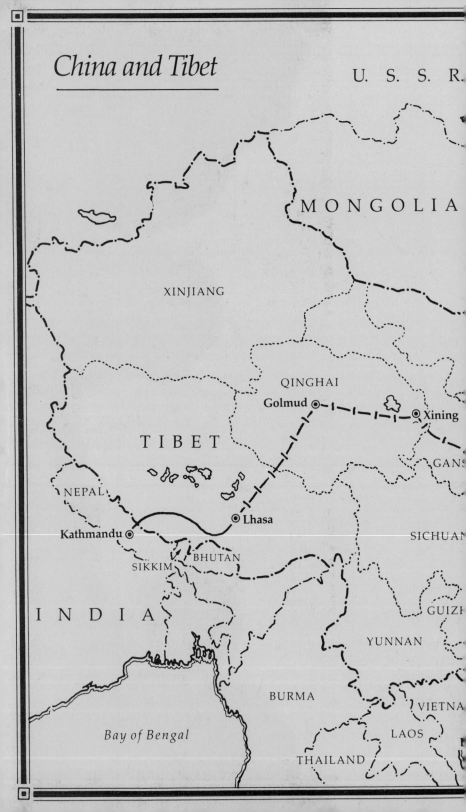

China and Tibet